D1389203

The
Confessions
of a
Poacher

The nineteenth century reminiscences
of an exponent of the fine art of poaching.

Poaching is one of the fine arts - how 'fine' only the initiated know

First published in 1890

John Watson
Illustrated by James West

Old House Books
Moretonhampstead,
Devon
www.OldHouseBooks.co.uk

Old House Books produce facsimile copies of long out of print
books that we believe deserve a second innings. Our reprints of
detailed Victorian and Edwardian maps and guide books are of
interest to genealogists and local historians. Other titles have
been chosen to explore the 'why' and 'how' of life in years gone
by and are of interest to anyone who wishes to know a bit more
about the lives of our forebears.

For details of other Old House Books titles see the final pages of
this book and, for the most up to date illustrated information,
please visit our website (www.OldHouseBooks.co.uk)
or request a catalogue.

We promise not to bombard you with junk mail and we will
never sell your details to another business.

First published by The Leadenhall Press in 1890
This edition was published in 2003 by

Old House Books,

The Old Police Station,
Pound Street,
Moretonhampstead,
Newton Abbot,
Devon   TQ13 8PA   UK

Tel: 01647 440707 Fax: 01647 440202

info@OldHouseBooks.co.uk

www.OldHouseBooks.co.uk

Printed and bound in India

ISBN 1 873590 28 8

EDITORIAL NOTE.

HE poacher of these " Confessions " is no im-
aginary being. In the following pages I have
set down nothing but what has come within
his own personal experience; and, although the little book
is full of strange inconsistencies, I cannot, knowing the man,
call them by a harder name. Nature made old " Phil "
a Poacher, but she made him a Sportsman and a
Naturalist at the same time. I never met any man
who was in closer sympathy with the wild creatures
about him; and never dog or child came within his
influence but what was permanently attracted by his
personality. Although eighty years of age there is still
some of the old erectness in his carriage; some of the
old fire in his eyes. As a young man he was handsome,
though now his features are battered out of all original
conception. His silvery hair still covers a lion-like head,
and his tanned cheeks are hard and firm. If his life has
been a lawless one he has paid heavily for his wrong
doings. Great as a poacher, he must have been great
whatever he had been. In my boyhood he was the
hero whom I worshipped, and I hardly know that I
have gone back on my loyalty.

CONTENTS.

CHAPTER.   PAGE.

1. THE EMBRYO POACHER -   -   -   -   -   7

2. UNDER THE NIGHT   -   -   -   -   -   19

3. GRADUATING IN WOODCRAFT -   -   -   -   32

4. PARTRIDGE POACHING   -   -   -   -   -   45

5. HARE POACHING   -   -   -   -   -   -   57

6. PHEASANT POACHING   -   -   -   -   -   74

7. SALMON AND TROUT POACHING   -   -   -   90

8. GROUSE POACHING -   -   -   -   -   -   109

9. RABBIT POACHING -   -   -   -   -   -   123

10. TRICKS -   -   -   -   -   -   -   -   135

11. PERSONAL ENCOUNTERS -   -   -   -   -   151

THE
CONFESSIONS OF A POACHER.

THE EMBRYO POACHER.

I DO not remember the time when I was not a poacher; and if I may say so, I believe our family has always had a genius for woodcraft.

I was bred on the outskirts of a sleepy town in a good game country, and my depredations were mostly when the Game Laws

B

were less rigorously enforced than now. Our home was roughly adorned in fur and feather, and a number of gaunt lurchers always constituted part of the family. An almost passionate love of nature, summers of birds' nesting, and a life spent almost wholly out of doors constituted an admirable training for an embryo poacher. If it is true that poets are born, not made, it is equally so of poachers. The successful "moucher" must be an inborn naturalist—must have much in common with the creatures of the fields and woods around him.

There is a miniature bird and animal fauna which constitutes as important game to the young poacher as any he is likely to come across in after life. There are mice, shrews, voles, for all of which he sets some primitive snare and captures. The silky-coated moles in their runs offer more serious work, and being most successfully practised at night, offers an additional charm. Then there are the red-furred squirrels which hide among the delicate leaves of the beeches and run up their

grey boles—fairy things that offer an endless
subject of delight to any young savage, and
their capturing draws largely upon his inventive
genius. A happy hunting ground is furnished
by farmers who require a lad to keep the birds
from their young wheat or corn, as when their
services are required the country is all like a
garden. At this time the birds seem creatures
born of the sun, and not only are they seen in
their brightest plumage, but when indulging in
all their love frolics. By being employed by
the farmers the erstwhile poacher is brought
right into the heart of the land, and the knowledge of woodcraft and rural life he there
acquires is never forgotten. As likely as not
a ditch runs by the side of the wheat
fields, and here the water-hen leads out
her brood. To the same spot the birds come
at noon to indulge their mid-day *siesta*, and in
the deep hole at the end of the cut a shoal of
silvery roach fall and rise towards the warm
sunlight. Or a brook, which is a tiny trout
stream, babbles on through the meadows and
pastures, and has its attractions too. A stream

is always the chief artery of the land, as in it
are found the life-giving elements. All the
birds, all the plants, flock to its banks, and its
wooded sides are hushed by the subdued hum
of insects. There are tall green brackens—
brackens unfurling their fronds to the light,
and full of the atoms of beautiful summer. At
the bend of the stream is a lime, and you may
almost see its glutinous leaves unfolding to
the light. Its winged flowers are infested with
bees. It has a
dead bough al-
most at the bot-
tom of its bole,
and upon it there
sits a grey-brown
bird. Ever and
anon it darts
for a moment,
hovers over the
stream, and then returns to its perch. A
hundred times it flutters, secures its insect
prey, and takes up its old position on the
stump. Bronze fly, bluebottle, and droning

THE SQUIRE'S KEEPER.

bee are secured alike, for all serve as food to the loveable pied fly-catcher.

It is the time of the bloom of the first June rose ; and here, by the margin of the wood, all the ground by fast falling blossom is littered. Every blade teems with life, and the air is instinct with the very breath of being. Birds' sounds are coming from over and under—from bough and brake, and a harmonious discord is flooded from the neighbouring copse. The oak above my head is a murmurous haunt of summer wings, and wood pigeons coo from the beeches. The air is still, and summer is on my cheek ; arum, wood-sorrel, and celandine mingle at my feet. The starlings are half buried in the fresh green grass, their metallic plumage flashing in the sun. Cattle are lazily lying dotted over the meadows, and the stream is done in a setting of green and gold. Swallows, skimming the pools, dip in the cool water, and are gone—leaving a sweet commotion in ever widening circles long after they have flown. A mouse-like creeper alights at the foot of a thorn, and runs nimbly up the bark ; midway it enters a hole in which is its nest. A garrulous blue-winged jay chatters from the tall oak, and purple rooks are picking among the corn. Butterflies dally through the warm air, and insects swarm among the leaves and flowers of the hedge bottoms. A crake calls, now here, now far out yonder. Blue-bells carpet the wood-margin, and the bog is bright with marsh plants.

This, then, is the workshop of the young poacher, and here he receives his first impressions. Is it strange that a mighty yearning springs up within him to know more of nature's secrets ? He finds himself in a fairy place, and all unconsciously drinks in its sweets. See him now deeply buried in a golden flood of marsh marigolds ! See how he stands spell-bound before saxifrages which cling to a dripping rock. Water avens, wild parsley, and campions crowd around him, and flags of the yellow and purple iris tower over all. He watches the doings of the reed-sparrows deep down in the flags, and sees a water-ouzel as it rummages among the pebbles at the

bottom of the brook. The larvæ of caddis
flies, which cover the edge of the stream, are
a curious mystery to him, and he sees the
kingfisher dart away as a bit of green light.
Small silvery trout, which rise in the pool,
tempt him to try for them with a crooked pin,
and even now with success. He hears the
cuckoos crying and calling as they fly from
tree to tree, and quite unexpectedly finds the
nest of a yellow-hammer, between a willow
and the bank, containing its curiouly speckled
eggs.

Still the life, and the "hush," and the
breath go on. Everything breathes, and
moves, and has its being ; the things of the
day are the essence thereof. On the margin
of the wood are a few young pines, their delicate plumes just touched with the loveliest
green. An odour of resinous gum is wafted
from them, and upon one of the slender sprays
a pair of diminutive goldcrests have hung their
procreant cradle. These things are enough to
win any young Bohemian to their ways,
and although as yet they only comprise "the

country," soon their wondrous detail lures
their lover on, and he seeks to satisfy the
thirst within him by night as well as by day.

Endless acquaintances are to be made
in the fields, and those of the most pleasurable description.   Nests containing young
squirrels can be found in the larch tree tops,
and any domestic tabby will suckle these
delightful playthings.   Young cushats and
cushats' eggs can be obtained from their
wicker-like nests, and sold in the villages.   A
prickly pet may be captured in a hedgehog
trotting off through the long grass, and colo-
nies of young wild rabbits may be dug from
the mounds and braes.   The skin of every
velvety mole is one patch nearer the accom-
plishment of a warm, furry vest for winter,
and this, if the pests of which it is comprised
are the owner's taking, is worn with pardonable
pride.   A moleskin vest constitutes a graduation in woodcraft so to speak.   Sometimes a
brace of leverets are found in a tussocky grass
clump, but these are more often allowed to
remain than taken.   And there are almost

innumerable captures to be made among the
feathered as well as furred things of the fields
and woods. Chaffinches are taken in nooses
among the corn, as are larks and buntings.
Crisp cresses from the springs constitute an
important source of income, and the embrowned
nuts of autumn a harvest in themselves. It is
during his early days of working upon the
land that the erstwhile
poacher learns of the
rain-bringing tides;
of the time of
migration of
birds; of the
evening gambol-
ing of hares; of
the coming to-
gether of the
partridge to
roost; of the
spawning of
salmon and
trout; and a hun-
dred other scraps

of knowledge which will serve him in good
stead in his subsequent protest against the
Game Laws.

Almost every young rustic who develops into
a poacher has some such outdoor education as
that sketched above.   He has about him
much ready animal ingenuity, and is capable
of almost infinite resource.   His snares and
lines are constructed with his pocket knife, out
of material he finds ready to hand in the woods.
He early learns to imitate the call of the game
birds, so accurately as to deceive even the
birds themselves ; and his weather-stained
clothes seem to take on themselves the duns
and browns and olives of the woods.   A child
brought up in the lap of Nature is invariably
deeply marked with her impress, and we shall
see to what end she has taught him.

Chapter 2

UNDER THE NIGHT.

Now came still evening on, and twilight gray
Had in her sober liv'ry all things clad.

WHEN the embryo poacher has once
tasted the forbidden fruits of the
land — and it matters not if his
game be but field-mice and squirrels—there is
only one thing wanting to win him completely
to Nature's ways. This is that he shall see
her sights and hear her sounds under the night.
There is a charm about the night side of nature
that the town dweller can never know.   I

have been once in London, and well remember what, as a country lad, impressed me
most.   It was the fact that I had, during the
small hours of the morning, stood alone on
London Bridge.   The great artery of life was
still ; the pulse of the city had ceased to beat.
Not a moving object was visible.   Although
bred among the lonely hills, I felt for the
first time that this was to be alone ; that
this was solitude.   I felt such a sense as
Macaulay's New Zealander may experience
when he sits upon the ruins of the same stu-
pendous structure ; and it was then for the
first time I knew whence the inspiration, and
felt the full force and realism of a line I had
heard, " O God ! the very houses seemed to
sleep."   I could detect no definite sound, only
that vague and distant hum that for ever
haunts and hangs over a great city.   Then
my thoughts flew homeward (to the fells and
upland fields, to the cold mists by the river, to
the deep and sombre woods).   I had never observed such a time of quiet there ; no absolute
and general period of repose.   There was

always something abroad, some creature of the fields or woods, which by its voice or movements was betrayed. Just as in an old rambling house there are always strange noises that cannot be accounted for, so in the night-paths of nature there are in-  numerable sounds which can never be localised. To those, however, who pursue night avocations in the country, there are always calls and cries which bespeak life as animate under the night as that of the day. This is attributable to various animals and birds, to beetles, to night-flying insects, even to fish ; and part of the education of the young poacher is to track these sounds to their source.

I have said that our family was a family of poachers. The old instinct was in us all, though I believe that the same wild spirit which drove us to the the moor and covert at night was only the same as was strongly implanted in the breast of Lord ————, our neighbour, who was a legitimate sportsman and a Justice of the Peace. If we were not allowed to see much real poaching when

we were young we saw a good deal of the preparations for it. As the leaves began to turn in autumn there was great activity in our old home among nets and snares. When wind and weather were favourable, late afternoon brought home my father, and his wires and nets were already spread on the clean sanded floor. There was a peg to sharpen, or a broken mesh to mend. Every now and then he would look out on the darkening night, always directing his glance upward. The two dogs would whine impatiently to be gone, and in an hour, with bulky pockets, he would start, striking right across the land and away from the high road. The dogs would prick out their ears on the track, but stuck doggedly to his heels ; and then, as we watched, the darkness would blot him out of the landscape, and we turned with our mother to the fireside. In summer we saw little but the " breaking " of the lurchers. These dogs take long to train, but, when perfected, are invaluable. All the best lurchers are the produce of a cross between the sheep-dog and greyhound, a combination which secures the speed and silence of the one, and the "nose" of the other. From the batches of puppies we always saved such as were rough-coated, as these were better able to stand the exposure of long, cold nights. In colour the best are fawn or brown—some shade which assimilates well to the duns and browns and yellows of the fields

c

and woods ; but our extended knowledge of the dogs came in after years.

The oak gun-rack in our old home contained a motley collection of fowling pieces, mostly with the barrels filed down. This was that the pieces might be more conveniently stowed away in the pocket until it was policy to have them out. The guns showed every graduation in age, size, and make, and among them was an old flint-lock which had been in the family for generations. This heirloom was often surreptitiously stolen away, and then we were able to bring down larger game. Wood pigeons were waited for in the larches, and shot as they came to roost. The crakes were called by the aid of a small "crank," and shot as they emerged from the lush summer grass. Large numbers of green plover were bagged from time to time, and often in winter we had a chance at their grey cousins, the whistling species. Both these fed in the water-meadows through winter, and the former were always abundant. In spring, "trips" of rare dotterel often led us about the higher hills for days, and sometimes we had to stay all night on the mountain. Then we were up with the first gray light in the morning, and generally managed to bring down a few birds. The feathers of these are extremely valuable for fishing, and my father invariably supplied them to the county justices who lived near us. He trained a dog to hunt dotterel, and so find their nests, and in this was most successful—more so than an eminent naturalist who spent five consecutive summers about the summits of our highest

mountains, though without ever coming across a nest or seeing the birds. Sometimes we bagged a gaunt heron as it flapped heavily from

a ditch—a greater fish poacher than any in the
country side. One of our great resorts on
winter evenings was to an island which bor-
dered a disused mill-dam. This was thickly
covered with aquatic vegetation, and to it
came teal, mallard, and poachard. All through
the summer we had worked assiduously at a
small " dug-out," and in this we waited, snugly
stowed away behind a willow root. When the
ducks appeared on the sky-line the old flint-
lock was out, a sharp report tore the darkness,
and a brace of teal or mallard floated down
stream, and on to the mill island. In this way
half a dozen ducks would be bagged, and, dead
or dying, they were left where they fell, and
retrieved next morning. Sometimes big game
was obtained in the shape of a brace of geese,
which proved themselves the least wary of a
flock ; but these only came in the severest
weather.

Cutting the coppice, assisting the charcoal
burners, or helping the old woodman—all gave
facilities for observing the habits of game, and
none of these opportunities were missed. In

this way we were brought right into the heart of the land, and our evil genius was hardly suspected. An early incident in the woods is worth recording. I have already said that we took snipe and woodcock by means of "gins" and "springes," and one morning on going to examine a snare, we discovered a large buzzard near one which was "struck." The bird endeavoured to escape, but, being evidently held fast, could not. A woodcock had been taken in one of our snares, which, while fluttering, had been seen and attacked by the buzzard. Not content, however, with the body of the woodcock, it had swallowed a leg also, around which the nooze was drawn, and the limb was so securely lodged in its stomach that no force which the bird could exert could withdraw it. The gamekeepers would employ us to take hedgehogs, which we did in steel traps baited with eggs. These prickly little animals were justly blamed for robbing pheasants' nests, and many a one paid the penalty for so doing. We received so much per head for the capture of these, as also for moles which tunnelled the

banks of the water meadows.   Being injurious
to the stream sides and the young larches, the
farmers were anxious to rid these ; and one
summer we received a commission to exercise
our knowledge of field-craft against them.   But
in the early days our greatest successes were
among the sea ducks and wildfowl which
haunted the marram-covered flats and ooze
banks of an inland bay a few miles from our
home.   Mention of our capturing the sea
birds brings to mind some very early rabbit
poaching.   At dusk the rabbits used to come
down from the woods, and on to the sandy sa-
line tracts to nibble the short sea grass.   As
twilight came we used to lie quiet among the
rocks and boulders, and, armed with the old
flint-lock, knock over the rabbits as soon as
they had settled to feed.   But this was only
tasting the delights of that first experience in
" fur " which was to become so widely developed in future years.   Working a duck
decoy—when we knew where we had the
decoyman—was another profitable night ad-
venture, which sometimes produced dozens

of delicate teal, mallard and widgeon. Another successful method of taking seafowl was by the " fly " or " ring " net. When there was but little or no moon these were set across the banks last covered by the tide. The nets were made of fine thread, and hung on poles from ten to twenty yards apart. Care had to be taken to do this loosely, so as to give the nets plenty of " bag." Sometimes we had these nets hung for half a mile along the mud flats, and curfew, whimbrel, geese, ducks, and various shore-haunting birds were taken in them. Sometimes a bunch of teal, flying down wind, would break right through the net and escape. This, however, was not a frequent occurrence.

There is one kind of poaching, which, as a lad, I was forbidden, and I have never indulged in it from that day to this. This was egg poaching. In our own district it was carried on to a large extent, though I never heard of it until the artificial rearing of game came in. The squire's keeper will give six-pence each for pheasants' eggs, and fourpence

for those of partridges. I know for certain
that he often buys eggs (unknowingly, of
course) from his master's preserves as well as
those of his neighbours. In the hedge bottom,
along the covert side, or among broom and
gorse, the farm labourer notices a pair of
partridges roaming morning after morning.
Soon he finds their oak-leaf nest and olive
eggs. These the keeper readily buys, winking
at what he knows to be dishonest. Plough-
boys and farm labourers have peculiarly favourable opportunities for egg poaching. As
to pheasants' eggs, if the keeper be an honest
man and refuses to buy, there are always large
town dealers who will. Once in the coverts
pheasants' eggs are easily found. The birds
get up heavily from their nests, and go away
with a loud whirring of wings. In this species
of poaching women and children are largely
employed, and at the time the former are os-
tensibly gathering sticks, the latter wild flowers.
I have known the owner of the " smithy," who
was the receiver in our village, send to London
in the course of a week a thousand eggs, every

one of them gathered off the neighbouring estates.

When I say that I never indulged in egg poaching I do not set up for being any better than my neighbours. I had been forbidden to do it as a lad because my father give it the ugly name of thieving, and it had never tempted me aside. It was tame work at best, and there was none of the exhilarating fascination about it that I found in going after the game birds themselves.

Chapter. 3

GRADUATING IN WOODCRAFT.

We hear the cry
  Of their voices high,
Falling dreamily through the sky ;
  But their forms we cannot see.

*J*UST as the sportsman loves "rough shooting," so the poacher invariably chooses wild ground for his depredations. There is hardly a sea-parish in the country which has not its shore shooter, its poacher, and its fowler. Fortunately for my graduation in woodcraft I fell in with one of the latter at the very time I most needed his instructions. As the "Snig," as I was generally called, was so passionately fond of "live" things, old "Kittiwake" was quite prepared to

be companionable. Although nearly three
score years and ten divided our lives, there
was something in common between us. Love
of being abroad beneath the moon and stars ;
of wild wintry skies ; of the weird cries that
came from out the darkness—love of everything indeed that pertained to the night side
of nature. What terrible tales of the sands
and marshes the old man would tell as we sat
in his turf-covered cottage, listening to the
lashing storm and driving water without. Occasionally we heard sounds of the Demon
Huntsman and his Wish-hounds as they crossed
the wintry skies. If Kittiwake knew, he would
never admit that these were the wild swans
coming from the north, which chose the
darkest nights for their migration. When my
old tutor saw that I was already skilled in the
use of " gins " and " springes," and sometimes
brought in a snipe or woodcock, his old
eyes glistened as he looked upon the marsh-
birds. It was on one such occasion, pleased
at my success, that he offered what he had
never offered to mortal—to teach me the whole

art of fowling.   I remember the old man as he lay on his heather bench when he made this magnanimous offer.   In appearance he was a splendid type of a northern yeoman, his face fringed with silvery hair, and cut in the finest features.   One eye was bright and clear even at his great age, though the other was rheumy, and almost blotted out.   He rarely undressed at nights, his outward garb seemed more a production of nature than of art, and was changed, when, like the outer cuticle of the marsh vipers, it sloughed off.   It was only in winter that the old man lived his lonely life on the mosses and marshes, for during the summer he turned from fowler to fisher, or assisted in the game preserves.   The haunts and habits of the marsh and shore birds he knew by heart, and his great success in taking them lay in the fact that he was a close and accurate observer. He would watch the fowl, then set his nets and noozes by the light of his acquired knowledge. These things he had always known, but it was in summer, when he was assisting at pheasant rearing, that he got to know all about game

in fur and feather. He noted that the handsome cock pheasants always crowed before
they flew up to roost ; that in the evening the
partridges called as they came together in the
grass lands; and he watched the ways of the
hares as they skipped in the moonlight. These
things we were wont to discuss when wild
weather prevented our leaving the hut ; and
all our plans were tested by experiment before
they were put into practice. It was upon
these occasions, too, that the garrulous old
man would tell of his early life. That was the
time for fowl ; but now the plough had in-
vaded the sea-birds' haunt. He would tell of
immense flocks of widgeon, of banks of brent
geese, and clouds of dunlin. Bitterns used to
boom and breed in the bog, and once, though
only once, a great bustard was shot. In his
young days Kittiwake had worked a decoy, as
had his father and grandfather before him ;
and when any stray fowler or shore-shooter
told of the effect of a single shot of their big
punt-guns, he would cap their stories by
going back to the days of decoying. Although

decoying had almost gone out, this was the only subject that the old man was reticent upon, and he surrounded the craft with all the mystery he was able to conjure up. The site of his once famous decoy was now drained, and in summer ruddy corn waved above it. Besides myself, Kittiwake's sole companion on the mosses was an old shaggy galloway, and it was almost as eccentric and knowing as its master. So great was the number of gulls and terns that bred on the mosses, that for two months during the breeding season the old horse was fed upon their eggs. Morning and evening a basketful was collected, and so long as these lasted Dobbin's coat continued sleek and soft.

In August and September we would capture immense numbers of " flappers "—plump wild ducks—but, as yet, unable to fly. These were either caught in the pools, or chased into nets which we set to intercept them. As I now took more than my share of the work, and made all the gins, springes, and noozes which we used, a rough kind of partnership sprung up between us.   The young ducks brought us good prices, and there was another source of income which paid well, but was not of long duration.   There is a short period in each year when even the matured wild ducks are quite unable to fly.   The male of the common wild duck is called the mallard, and soon after his brown duck begins to sit the drake moults the whole of its flight feathers.   So sudden and simultaneous is this process that for six weeks in summer the usually handsome drake is quite incapable of flight, and it is probably at this period of its ground existence that the assumption of the duck's plumage is such an aid to protection.   Quite the handsomest of the wildfowl on the marsh were a colony of sheldrakes which occupied a number of disused rabbit-burrows on a raised plateau overlooking the bay.   The ducks were bright chestnut, white, and purple, and in May laid from nine to a dozen creamy eggs.   As these birds brought high prices for stocking ornamental waters, we used to collect the eggs and hatch them out under hens in the turf cottage.   This

was a quite successful experiment up to a
certain point ; but the young fowl, immediately
they were hatched, seemed to be able to smell
the salt water, and would cover miles to gain
the creek.   With all our combined watchfulness the downy ducklings sometimes suc-
seeded in reaching their loved briny element,
and once in the sea were never seen again.
The pretty sea swallows used to breed on the
marsh, and the curious ruffs and reeves.   These
indulged in the strangest flights at breeding
time, and it was then that we used to capture
the greatest numbers.   We took them alive in
nets, and then fattened them on soaked wheat.
The birds were sent all the way to London,
and brought good prices.   By being kept
closely confined and frequently fed, in a fortnight they became so plump as to resemble
balls of fat, and then brought as much as
a florin a piece.   If care were not taken to kill
the birds just when they attained to their
greatest degree of fatness they fell rapidly in
condition, and were nearly worthless.   To kill
them we were wont to pinch off the head, and

when all the blood had exuded the flesh remained white and delicate. Greater delicacies even than ruffs and reeves were godwits, which were fatted in like manner for the table. Experiments in fattening were upon one occasion succesfully tried with a brood of greylag geese which we discovered on the marshes. As this is the species from which the domestic stock is descended, we found little difficulty in herding, though we were always careful to house them at night, and pinioned them as the time of the autumnal migration came round. We well knew that the skeins of wild geese which at this time nightly cross the sky, calling as they fly, would soon have robbed us of our little flock.

In winter, snipe were always numerous on the mosses, and were among the first birds to be affected by severe weather. If on elevated ground when the frost set in, they immediately betake themselves to the lowlands, and at these times we used to take them in pantles made of twisted horsehair. In preparing these we trampled a strip of oozy ground until, in the

D

darkness, it had the appearance of a narrow plash of water. The snipe were taken as they came to feed on ground presumably containing food of which they were fond. As well as woodcock and snipe, we took larks by thousands. The pantles for these we set somewhat differently than those intended for the minor game birds. A main line, sometimes as much as a hundred yards in length, was set along the marsh ; and to this at short intervals were attached a great number of loops of horsehair in which the birds were strangled. During the migratory season, or in winter when larks are flocked, sometimes a hundred bunches of a dozen each would be taken in a single day.

During the rigour of winter great flocks of migratory ducks and geese came to the bay, and prominent among them were immense flocks of scoters. Often from behind an ooze bank did we watch parties of these playing and chasing each other over the crests of the waves, seeming indifferent to the roughest seas. The coming of the scoter brought flush times, and in hard weather our takes were tremendous. Another of the wild ducks which visited us was the pochard or dunbird. We mostly called it "poker" and "redhead," owing to the bright chestnut of its neck and head. It is somewhat heavily made, swims low in the water, and from its legs being placed far behind for diving it is very awkward on land. In winter the pochard was abundant on the coast, but as it was one of the shyest of fowl it was always difficult to approach. If alarmed it paddles rapidly away, turning its head, and always keeping an eye to the rear. On account of its wariness it is oftener netted than shot. The shore-shooters hardly ever get a chance at it. We used to take it in the creeks on the marsh, and, as the matter is difficult to explain, I will let the following quotation tell how it was done :

" The water was surrounded with huge nets, fastened with poles laid flat on the ground when ready for action, each net being, perhaps, sixty feet long and twenty feet deep. When all was ready the pochards were frightened off the water. Like all diving ducks they were obliged to fly low for some distance, and also to head the wind before rising. Just as the mass of birds reached the side of the pool, one of the immense nets, previously regulated by weights and springs, rose upright as it was freed from its fastenings by the fowler from a distance with a long rope. If this were done at the right moment the ducks were met full in the face by a wall of net, and thrown helpless into a deep ditch dug at its foot for their reception."

In addition to our nets and snares we had a primitive fowling-piece, though we only used it when other methods failed. It was an ancient flint-lock, with tremendously long barrels. Sometimes it went off; oftener it did not. I well remember with what desperation I, upon one occasion, clung to this murderous weapon whilst it meditated, so to speak. It is true that it brought down quite a wisp of dunlins, but then there was almost a cloud of them to fire at. These and golden plover were mainly the game for the flint-lock, and with them we were peculiarly successful. If we had not been out all night we were invariably abroad at dawn, when golden plover fly and feed in close bodies. Upon these occasions sometimes a dozen birds were bagged at a shot, though, after all, the chief product of our days were obtained in the cymbal nets. We invariably used a decoy, and when the wild birds were brought down, and came within the workings of the net, it was rapidly pulled over and the game secured. For the most part, however, only the smaller birds were taken in this way. Coots came round in their season, and although they yielded a good harvest, netting them was not very profitable, for as their flesh was dark and fishy only the villagers and fisher-folk would buy them.

A curious little bird, the grebe or dabchick, used to haunt the pools and ditches of the marsh, and we not unfrequently caught them in the nets whilst drawing for salmon which ran up the creek to spawn. They had curious feet, lobed like chestnut leaves, and hardly any wing. This last was more like a flipper, and upon one occasion, when no less than three had caught in the meshes, a dispute arose between us as to whether they were able to fly. Kittiwake and I argued that whilst they were resident and bred in the marshes, yet their numbers were greatly augmented in autumn by other birds which came to spend the winter. Whilst I contended that they flew, Kittiwake said that their tiny wings could never support them, and certainly neither of us had ever seen them on their journeyings. Two of the birds we took a mile from the water, and then threw them into the air, when they darted off straight and swift for the mosses which lay stretched at our feet a mile below.

Chapter 4.

PARTRIDGE POACHING.

THE bloom on the brambles; the ripening of the nuts; and the ruddiness of the corn all acted as reminders that the "fence" time was rapidly drawing to a close. So much did the first frosts quicken us that it was dfficult to resist throwing up our farm work before the game season was fairly upon us. There was only one way in which we could curb the wild impulse within. We stood up to the golden corn and smote it from the rising to the going down of the sun. The hunters' moon tried

hard to win us to the old hard life of sport ;
but still the land must be cleared.   There was
a double pleasure in the ruddy sheaves, for
they told of golden guineas, and until the
last load was carried neither nets, gins, nor the
old duck-gun were of any use.   The harvest
housed the game could begin, and then the
sweet clover, which the hares loved, first
pushed their shoots between the stubble stalks.
But neither the hares on the fallows, the
grouse on the moor, nor the pheasants on the
bare branches brought us so much pleasure as
the partridge.   A whole army of shooters love
the little brown birds, and we are quite of
their way of thinking.

A long life of poaching has not cooled our
ardour for this phase of woodcraft.   At the out-
set we may state that we have almost invariably
observed close times, and have rarely killed a
hare or game-bird out of season.   The man
who excels in poaching must be country bred.
He must not only know the land, but the
ways of the game by heart.   Every sign of
wind and weather must be observed, as all

help in the silent trade. Then there is the rise and wane of the moon, the rain-bringing tides, and the shifting of the birds with the seasons. These and a hundred other things must be kept in an unwritten calendar, and only the poacher can keep it. Speaking from hard experience, his out-door life will make him quick; will endow him with much ready animal ingenuity. He will take in an immense amount of knowledge of the life of the fields and woods; and it is this teaching which will ultimately give him accuracy of eye and judgment sufficient to interpret what he sees aright. To succeed the poacher must be a specialist. It is better if he directs his attention to "fur," or to "feather" alone; but it is terribly hard to resist going in for both. There is less scope for field ingenuity in taking game birds; but at the same time there is always the probability of more wholesale destruction. This arises from the fact of the birds being gregarious. Both grouse and partridge go in coveys, and pheasants are found in the company of their own kind. Partridges roost on

the ground, and sleep with tails tucked
together and heads outwards. Examine the
fallow after they have left it in a morning, and
this will be at once apparent. A covey in this
position represents little more than a mass of
feathers. It is for protective reasons that
partridges always spend their nights in the
open. Birds which do not perch would soon
become extinct were they to seek the protection of woods and hedge-bottoms by night.
Such ground generally affords cover for
vermin—weazels, polecats, and stoats. Although partridges roam far by day, they
invariably come together at night, being par-
tial to the same fields and fallows. They run
much, and rarely fly, except when passing from
one feeding ground to another. In coming
together in the evening their calls may be
heard to some distance. These were the
sounds we listened for, and marked. We re-
membered the gorse bushes, and knew that
the coveys would not be far from them.

We always considered partridge good game,
and sometimes were watching a dozen coveys

at the same time. September once in, there was never a sun-down that did not see one of us on our rounds making mental notes. It was not often, however, that more than three coveys were marked for a night's work. One of these, perhaps, would be in turnips, another among stubble, and the third on grass. According to the nature of the crop, the lay of the land, wind, &c., so we varied our tactics. Netting partridges always requires two persons, though a third to walk after the net is helpful. If the birds have been carefully marked down, a narrow net is used ; if their roosting-place is uncertain a wider net is better. When all is ready this is slowly dragged along the ground, and is thrown down immediately the whirr of wings is heard. If neatly and silently done, the whole covey is bagged. There is a terrible flutter, a cloud of brown feathers, and all is over. It is not always, however, that the draw is so successful. In view of preventing this method of poaching, especially on land where many partridges roost, keepers plant low scrubby thorns at intervals. These so far interfere with the working of the net as to allow the birds time to escape. We were never much troubled, however, in this way. As opportunity offered the quick-thorns were torn up, and a dead black-thorn bough took their place. As the thorns were low the difference was never noticed, even by the keepers, and, of course, they were carefully removed before, and replaced after, netting. Even when the dodge was detected the fields and fallows had been pretty much stripped of the birds. This method is impracticable now, as the modern method of reaping leaves the brittle stubble as bare as the squire's lawn. We had always a great objection to use a wide net where a narrow one would suit the purpose. Among turnips, and where large numbers of birds were supposed to lie, a number of rows or " riggs " were taken at a time, until the whole of the ground had been traversed. This last method is one that requires time and a knowledge of the keeper's beat. On rough ground the catching of the net may be obviated by having about eighteen inches of smooth glazed material bordering the lowest and trailing part of it. Some of the small farmers were as fond of poaching as ourselves, and here is a trick which one of them successfully employed whenever he heard the birds in his land. He scattered a train of grain from the field in which the partridge roosted, each morning bringing it nearer and nearer to the stack-yard. After a time the birds became accustomed to this mode of feeding, and as they grew bolder the grain-train was continued inside the barn. When they saw the golden feast invitingly spread, they were not slow to enter, and the doors were quickly closed upon them. Then the farmer entered with a bright light and felled the birds with a stick.

In the dusk of a late autumn afternoon a splendid " pot " shot was sometimes had at a bunch of partridges just gathered for the night. I remember a score such. The call of the partridge is less deceptive than any other game bird, and the movements of a covey are easily watched. This tracking is greatly aided if the field in which the birds are is bounded by stone walls. As dusk deepens and draws to dark, they run and call less, and soon all is still. The closely-packed covey is easy to detect against the yellow stubble, and resting the gun on the wall, a charge of heavy shot fired into their midst usually picks off the lot. If in five minutes the shot brings up the keeper it matters little, as then you are far over the land.

Partridges feed in the early morning—as soon as day breaks, in fact. They resort to one spot, and are constant in their coming, especially if encouraged. This fact I well knew, and laid my plans accordingly. By the aid of the moon a train of grain was laid straight as a hazel wand. Upon these occasions I never went abroad without an old duck-gun, the barrels of which had been filed down. This enabled me to carry the gun-stock in one pocket, the barrels in the other. The shortness of the latter in nowise told against the shooting, as the gun was only required to use at short distances. The weapon was old, thick at the muzzle, and into it I crammed a heavy charge of powder and shot. Ensconced in the scrub I had only now to wait for the dawn. Almost before it was fully light the covey would come with a loud whirring of wings, and settle to feed immediately. This was the critical moment. Firing along the line a single shot strewed the ground with dead and dying ; and in ten minutes, always keeping clear of the roads, I was a mile from the spot.

I had yet another and a more successful method of taking partridges. When, from the watchfulness or cleverness of keepers (they are not intelligent men as a rule), both netting and shooting proved impracticable, I soaked grain until it became swollen, and then steeped it in the strongest spirit. This, as before, was strewn in the morning paths of the partridge, and, soon taking effect, the naturally pugnacious birds were presently staggering and fighting desperately. Then I bided my time, and as opportunity offered, knocked the incapacitated birds on the head.

One of the most ingenious and frequently successful methods I employed for bagging

partridge was by the aid of an old setter
bitch having a lantern tied to her neck.

Being somewhat risky, I only employed it
when other plans failed, and when I had a
good notion of the keeper's whereabouts.
The lantern was made from an old salmon
canister stripped of its sides, and contained a
bit of candle. When the bitch was put off
into seeds or stubble she would range quietly
until she found the birds, then stand as

stiffly as though done in marble. This shewed me just where the covey lay, and as the light either dazzled or frightened the birds, it was not difficult to clap the net over them. It sometimes happened that others besides myself were watching this strange luminous light, and it was probably set down as some phenomenon of the night-side of nature. Once, however, I lost my long silk net, and as there was everything to be gained by running, and much

to be lost by staying, I ran desperately. Only an old, slow dog can be used in this species of poaching, and it is marvellous to see with what spirit and seeming understanding it enters into the work.

Chapter 5.

Hare Poaching.

The merry brown hares came leaping
Over the crest of the hill,
Where the clover and corn lay sleeping
Under the moonlight still.

OUR hare season generally began with partridge poaching, so that the coming of the hunter's moon was always an interesting autumnal event. By its aid the first big bag of the season was made. When a field is sown down, which it is intended to bring back to grass, clover is invariably sown

with the grain. This springs between the corn
stalks, and by the time the golden sheaves are
carried, has swathed the stubble with mantling
green. This, before all others, is the crop
which hares love.

Poaching is one of the fine arts, and the
man who would succeed must be a specialist. If
he has sufficient strength to refrain from general
"mouching," he will succeed best by selecting
one particular kind of game, and directing his
whole knowledge of woodcraft against it. In
spring and summer I was wont to closely scan
the fields, and as embrowned September drew
near, knew the whereabouts of every hare in
the parish—not only the field where it lay,
but the very clump of rushes in which was its
form. As puss went away from the gorse, or
raced down the turnip-rigg, I took in every
twist and double down to the minutest detail.

Then I scanned the "smoots" and gates
through which she passed, and was always
careful to approach these laterally. I left no
trace of hand nor print of foot, nor disturbed
the rough herbage. Late afternoon brought

me home, and upon the hearth the wires and nets were spread for inspection. When all was ready, and the dogs whined impatiently to be gone, I would strike right into the heart of the land, and away from the high-road.

Mention of the dogs brings me to my fastest friends Without them poaching for fur would be almost impossible. I invariably used bitches, and as success depended almost wholly upon them, I was bound to keep only the best. Lurchers take long to train, but when perfected are invaluable. I have had, maybe, a dozen dogs in all, the best being the result of a pure cross between greyhound and sheepdog. In night work silence is essential to success, and such dogs never bark ; they have the good nose of the one, and the speed of the other. In selecting puppies it is best to choose rough-coated ones, as they are better able to stand the exposure of cold, rough nights. Shades of brown and fawn are preferable for colour, as these best assimilate to the duns and browns of the fields and woods. The process of training would take

long to describe ; but it is wonderful how soon
the dog takes on the habits of its master. They

soon learn to slink along by hedge and ditch,
and but rarely shew in the open.   They know

every field-cut and by-path for miles, and are as much aware as their masters that county constables have a nasty habit of loitering about unfrequented lanes at daybreak.

The difficulty lies not so much in obtaining game as in getting it home safely ; but for all that I was but rarely surprised with game upon me in this way. Disused buildings, stacks, and dry ditches are made to contain the "haul" until it can be sent for—an office which I usually got some of the field-women to perform for me. Failing these, country carriers and early morning milk-carts were useful. When I was night poaching, it was important that I should have the earliest intimation of the approach of a possible enemy, and to secure this the dogs were always trained to run on a few hundred yards in advance. A well-trained lurcher is almost infallible in detecting a foe, and upon meeting one he runs back to his master under cover of the *far side* of a fence. When the dog came back to me in this way I lost not a second in accepting the shelter of the nearest hedge or deepest ditch till the danger was past. If suddenly surprised and without means of hiding, myself and the dog would make off in different directions. Then there were times when it was inconvenient that we should know each other, and upon such occasions the dogs would not recognise me even upon the strongest provocation.

My best lurchers knew as much of the habits of game as I did. According to the class of land to be worked they were aware whether hares, partridges, or rabbits were to constitute the game for the night. They judged to a nicety the speed at which a hare should be driven to make a snare effective, and acted accordingly. At night the piercing scream of a netted hare can be heard to a great distance, and no sound sooner puts the keeper on the alert.

Consequently, when "puss" puts her neck into a wire, or madly jumps into a gate-net, the dog is on her in an instant, and quickly stops her piteous squeal. In field-netting rabbits, lurchers are equally quick, seeming quite to appreciate the danger of noise. Once only have I heard a lurcher give mouth. "Rough"

was a powerful, deep-chested bitch, but upon one occasion she failed to jump a stiff,
stone fence, with a nine-pound hare in her
mouth. She did not bark, however, until she
had several times failed at the fence, and when
she thought her whereabouts were unknown.
Hares and partridges invariably squat on the
fallow or in the stubble when alarmed, and remain absolutely still till the danger is passed.
This act is much more likely to be observed
by the dog than its master, and in such cases
the lurchers gently rubbed my shins to apprise
me of the fact. Then I moved more cautiously. Out-lying pheasants, rabbits in the
clumps, red grouse on the heather—the old
dog missed none of them. Every movement
was noted, and each came to the capacious
pocket in turn. The only serious fights I ever
had were when keepers threatened to shoot
the dogs. This was a serious matter. Lurchers
take long to train, and a keeper's summary
proceeding often stops a whole winter's work,
as the best dogs cannot easily be replaced.
Many a one of our craft would as soon have

been shot himself as seen his dog destroyed;
and there are few good dogs which have not,
at one time or other, been riddled with pellets
during their lawless (save the mark!) career.
If a hare happens to be seen, the dog sometimes works it so cleverly as to ".chop" it in
its "form"; and both hares and rabbits are not
unfrequently snapped up without being run
at all.   In fact, depredations in fur would be
exceedingly limited without the aid of dogs;
and one country squire saved his ground game
for a season by buying my best brace of lurchers at a very fancy price; while upon another
occasion a bench of magistrates demanded to
see the dogs of whose doings they had heard
so much.   In short, my lurchers at night em-
bodied all my senses.

Whilst preparing my nets and wires, the
dogs would whine impatiently to be gone.
Soon their ears were pricked out on the track,
though until told to leave they stuck doggedly
to heel. Soon the darkness would blot out
even the forms of surrounding objects, and our
movements were made more cautiously.   A

couple of snares are set in gaps in an old
thorn fence not more than a yard apart These
are delicately manipulated, as we know from
previous knowledge that the hare will take one
of them. The black dog is sent over, the
younger fawn bitch staying behind. The
former slinks slowly down the field, sticking
close to the cover of a fence running at right
angles to the one in which the wires are set.
I have arranged that the wind shall blow from
the dog and across to the hare's seat when the
former shall come opposite. The ruse acts;
"puss" is alarmed, but not terrified ; she gets
up and goes quietly away for the hedge. The
dog is crouched, anxiously watching ; she is
making right for the snare, though something
must be added to her speed to make the wire
effective. As the dog closes in, I wait, bowed,
with hands on knees, still as death, for her
coming. I hear the brush of the grass,
the trip, trip, trip, as the herbage is brushed.
There is a rustle among the dead leaves,
a desperate rush, a momentary squeal—and the
wire has tightened round her throat.

Again we trudge silently along the lane, but soon stop to listen. Then we disperse, but to any on-looker would seem to have dissolved. This dry ditch is capacious, and its dead herbage tall and tangled. A heavy foot, with regular beat, approaches along the road, and dies slowly away in the distance.

Hares love green cornstalks, and a field of young wheat is at hand ; I spread a net, twelve feet by six, at the gate, and at a sign the dogs depart different ways. Their paths soon converge, for the night is torn by a piteous cry ; the road is enveloped in a cloud of dust ; and in the midst of the confusion the dogs dash over the fence. They must have found their game near the middle of the field, and driven the hares—for there are two—so hard that they carried the net right before them ; every struggle wraps another mesh about them, and, in a moment, their screams are quieted. By a quick movement I wrap the long net about my arm, and, taking the noiseless sward, get hastily away from the spot.

In March, when hares are pairing, four or five may frequently be found together in one field. Although wild, they seem to lose much of their natural timidity, and during this month I usually reaped a rich harvest. I was always careful to set my wires and snares on the side *opposite* to that from which the game would come, for this reason—that hares approach any place through which they are about to pass in a zig-zag manner. They come on, playing and frisking, stopping now and then to nibble the herbage. Then they canter, making wide leaps at right angles to their path, and sit listening upon their haunches. A freshly impressed footmark, the scent of dog or man, almost invariably turns them back. Of course these traces are certain to be left if the snare be set on the *near* side of the gate or fence, and then a hare will refuse to take it, even when hard pressed. Now here is a wrinkle to any keeper who cares to accept it. Where poaching is prevalent and hares abundant, *every hare on the estate should be netted*, for it is a fact well known to every poacher versed in his craft, that an escaped hare that has once been netted can never be retaken. The process, however, will effectually frighten a small percentage of hares off the land altogether.

The human scent left at gaps and gateways by ploughmen, shepherds, and mouchers, the

wary poacher will obliterate by driving sheep over the spot before he begins operations. On the sides of fells and uplands hares are difficult to kill. This can only be accomplished by swift dogs, which are taken *above* the game. Puss is made to run down-hill, when, from her peculiar formation, she goes at a disadvantage.

Audacity almost invariably stands the poacher in good stead. Here is an actual incident. I knew of a certain field of young wheat in which was several hares—a fact observed during the day   This was hard by the keeper's cottage, and surrounded by a high fence of loose stones. It will be seen that the situation was somewhat critical, but that night my nets were set at the gates through which the hares always made. To drive them the dog was to range the field, entering it at a point furthest away from the gate. I bent my back in the road a yard from the wall to aid the dog. It retired, took a mighty spring, and barely touching my shoulders, bounded over the fence. The risk was justified by the haul, for that night I bagged nine good hares.

Owing to the scarcity of game, hare-poaching is now hardly worth following, and I believe that what is known as the *Ground*

Game Act is mainly responsible for this.   A
country Justice, who has often been my friend
when I was sadly in need of one, asked me
why I thought the Hares and Rabbits Act
had made both kinds of fur scarcer.   I told
him that the hare would become abundant
again if it were not beset by so many enemies.
Since 1880 it has had no protection, and
the numbers have gone down amazingly.   A
shy and timid animal, it is worried through
every month of the year.   It does not
burrow, and has not the protection of the
rabbit.   Although the colour of its fur re-
sembles that of the dead grass and herbage
among which it lies, yet it starts from its
" form " at the approach of danger, and from
its size makes an easy mark.   It is not unfrequently " chopped " by sheep-dogs, and in
certain months hundreds of leverets perish in
this way.   Hares are destroyed wholesale
during the mowing of the grass and the reaping
of the corn.   For a time in summer, leverets
especially seek this kind of cover, and farmers
and farm-labourers kill numbers with dog and

gun—and this at a time when they are quite unfit
for food. In addition to these causes of scarcity
there are others well known to sportsmen.
When harriers hunt late in the season—as they
invariably do now-a-days—many leverets are
" chopped," and for every hare that goes
away three are killed in the manner in-
dicated. At least, that is my experience
while mouching in the wake of the hounds.
When hunting continues through March,
master and huntsman assert that this havoc is
necessary in order to kill off superabundant
jack-hares, and so preserve the balance of
stock. Doubtless there was reason in this
argument before the present scarcity, but now
there is none. March, too, is a general
breeding month, and the hunting of doe-hares
entails the grossest cruelty. Coursing is
confined within no fixed limits, and is pro-
longed far too late in the season. What has
been said of hunting applies to coursing, and
these things sportsmen can remedy if they
wish. There is more unwritten law in connection with British field-sports than any other

F

pastime ; but obviously it might be added to
with advantage.   If something is not done the
hare will assuredly become extinct.   To prevent this a "close time" is, in the opinion
of those best versed in woodcraft, absolutely
necessary.   The dates between which the
hare would best be protected are the first
of March and the first of August.   Then we
would gain all round.   The recent relaxation
of the law has done something to encourage
poaching, and poachers now find pretexts for
being on or about land which before were of
no avail, and to the moucher accurate observation by day is one of the essentials to
success.

Naturalists ought to know best ; but there has
been more unnatural history written concerning
hares than any other British animal.   It is said
to produce two young ones at a birth, but ob-
servant poachers know that from three to five
leverets are not unfrequently found : then it is
stated that hares breed twice, or at most thrice,
a year.   Anyone, however, who has daily observed their habits, knows that there are but

few months in which leverets are not born.
In mild winters young ones are found in
January and February, whilst in March they
have become common. They may be seen
right on through summer and autumn, and last
December I saw a brace of leverets a month old.
Does shot in October are sometimes found to
be giving milk, and in November old hares are
not unfrequently noticed in the same patch of
cover. These facts would seem to point to
the conclusion that the hare propagates its
species almost the whole year round—a startling
piece of evidence to the older naturalists. Add
to this that hares pair when a year old, that
gestation lasts only thirty days, and it will be
seen what a possibly prolific animal the hare
may be. The young are born covered with
fur, and after a month leave their mother to
seek their own subsistence.

Chapter 6.

Pheasant Poaching.

THROUGH late summer and autumn the poacher's thoughts go out to the early weeks of October. Neither the last load of ruddy corn, nor the actual netting of the partridge gladden his heart as do the first signs of the dying year. There are certain sections of the Game Laws which he never breaks, and only some rare circumstance tempts him to take immature birds. But by the third week of October the yellow and sere of the year has come. The duns and browns are over the woods, and the leaves come fitfully flickering down. Everything out of doors testifies that autumn is waning, and that winter will soon be upon us. The colours of the few remaining flowers are fading, and nature is beginning to have a washed-out appearance. The feathery plumes of the ash are everywhere strewn beneath the trees, for, just as the ash is the first to burst into leaf, so it is the first to go. The foliage of the oak is already assuming a bright chestnut, though the leaves will remain throughout the year. In the oak avenues the acorns are lying in great quantities, though oak mast is not now the important product it once was, cheap grain having relegated it almost exclusively to the use of the birds. And now immense flocks of wood pigeons flutter in the trees or pick up the food from beneath. The garnering of the grain, the flocking of migratory birds, the wild clanging of fowl in the night sky—these are the sights and sounds that set the poacher's thoughts off in the old grooves.

Of all species of poaching, that which en-
sures a good haul of pheasants is most beset
with difficulty.   Nevertheless there are silent
ways and means which prove as successful in the
end as the squire's guns, and these without breaking the woodland silence with a sound.   The
most successful of these I intend to set down,
and only such will be mentioned as have stood
me in good stead in actual night work.   Among
southern woods and coverts the pheasant
poacher is usually a desperate character ; not
so in the north.   Here
the poachers are
more skilled in
woodcraft, and
are rarely sur-
prised.   If the
worst comes
to the
worst
it is a
fair
stand-up fight with fists, and is usually blood-
less.   There is little greed of gain in the night

enterprise, and liberty by flight is the first thing resorted to.

It is well for the poacher, and well for his methods, that the pheasant is rather a stupid bird. There is no gainsaying its beauty, however, and a brace of birds, with all the old excitement thrown in, are well worth winning, even at considerable risk. In a long life of poaching I have noticed that the pheasant has one great characteristic. It is fond of wandering; and this cannot be prevented. Watch the birds : even when fed daily, and with the daintiest food, they wander off, singly or in pairs, far from the home coverts. This fact I knew well, and was not slow to use my knowledge. When October came round they were the very first birds to which I directed my attention. Every poacher observes, year by year (even leaving his own predaceous paws out of the question), that it by no means follows that the man who rears the pheasants will have the privilege of shooting them. There is a very certain time in the life of the bird when it disdains the scattered corn of the keeper, and begins to anticipate the fall of beech and oak mast. In search of this the pheasants make daily journeys, and consume great quantities. They feed principally in the morning ; dust themselves in the roads or turnip-fields at mid-day, and ramble through the woods in the afternoon. And one thing is certain : That when wandered birds find themselves in outlying copses in the evening they are apt to roost there. As already stated, these were the birds to which I paid my best attention. When wholesale pheasant poaching is prosecuted by gangs, it is in winter, when the trees are bare. Guns, with the barrels filed down, are taken in sacks, and the pheasants are shot where they roost. Their bulky forms stand sharply out-lined against the sky, and they are invariably on the lower branches. If the firing does not immediately bring up the keepers, the game is quickly deposited in bags, and the gang makes off. And it is generally arranged that a light cart is waiting at some remote lane end, so that possible pursuers may be quickly

outpaced. The great risk incurred by this
method will be seen, when it is stated that
pheasants are generally reared close by the
keeper's cottage, and that their coverts immediately surround it. It is mostly armed mouchers
who enter these, and not the
more gifted (save the mark !)
country poacher. And there
are reasons for this. Oppo-
sition must always be an-
ticipated, for, speaking
for the nonce from the
game - keeper's stand-
point, the covert never
should be, and rarely
is, unwatched. Then
there are the certain re-
sults of possible capture to
be taken into account. This
affected, and with birds in one's
possession, the poacher is liable
to be indicted upon so many concurrent charges,
each and all having heavy penalties. Than this
I obtained my game in a different and quieter

way.   My custom was to carefully eschew the
preserves, and look up all outlying birds. I never
went abroad without a pocketful of corn, and
day by day enticed the wandered birds further
and further away. This accomplished, pheasants
may be snared with hair nooses, or taken in
spring traps.   One of my commonest and most
successful methods with wandered birds was to
light brimstone beneath the trees in which they
roosted. The powerful fumes soon overpowered
them, and they came flopping down the trees
one by one.   This method has the advantage
of silence, and if the night be dead and still,
is rarely detected.   Away from the preserves,
time was never taken into account in my
plans, and I could work systematically.   I was
content with a brace of birds at a time, and
usually got most in the end, with least chance
of capture.

I have already spoken at some length of my
education in field and wood-craft.   An important (though at the time unconscious)
part of this was minute observation of the
haunts and habits of all kinds of game ; and

this knowledge was put to good use in my actual poaching raids. Here is an instance of what I mean : I had noticed the great pugnacity of the pheasant, and out of this made capital. After first finding out the whereabouts of the keeper, I fitted a trained game-cock with artificial spurs, and then took it to the covert side. The artificial spurs were fitted to the natural ones, were sharp as needles, and the plucky bird already knew how to use them. Upon his crowing, one or more cock pheasants would immediately respond, and advance to meet the adversary. A single blow usually sufficed to lay low the pride of the pheasant, and in this way half-a-dozen birds were bagged, whilst my own representative remained unhurt.

I had another ingenious plan (if I may say so) in connection with pheasants, and, perhaps, the most successful. I may say at once that there is nothing sportsmanlike about it ; but then that is in keeping with most of what I have set down. If time and opportunity offer there is hardly any limit to the depredation

which it allows.   Here it is : A number of
dried peas are taken and steeped in boiling
water ; a hole is then made through the centre,
and through this again a stiff bristle is threaded.
The ends are then cut off short, leaving only
about a quarter of an inch of bristle projecting
on each side.   With these the birds are fed,
and they are greedily eaten.   In passing down
the gullet, however, a violent irritation is
set up, and the pheasant is finally choked.
In a dying condition the birds are picked up
beneath the hedges, to the shelter of which
they almost always run.   The way is a quiet
one; it may be adopted in roads and lanes
where the birds dust themselves, and does
not require trespass.

In this connection I may say that I only
used a gun when every other method
failed.   Game-keepers sometimes try to outwit
poachers by a device which is now of old
standing.   Usually knowing from what quarter
the latter will enter the covert, wooden
blocks representing roosting birds are nailed
to the branches of the open beeches.   I was

never entrapped into firing at these dummies, and it is only with the casual that the ruse acts. He fires, brings the keepers from their hiding places, and is caught. Still another method of bagging "long-tails," though one somewhat similar to that already set down: It requires two persons, and the exact position of the birds must be known. A black night is necessary; a stiff bamboo rod, and a dark lantern. One man flashes the concentrated light upon the bare branches, when immediately half a dozen necks are stretched out to view the apparition. Just then the "angler" slips a wire nooze over the craned neck nearest him, and it is jerked down as quickly, though as silently as possible. Number two is served in like manner, then a third, a fourth, and a fifth. This method has the advantage of silence, though, if unskilfully managed, sometimes only a single bird is secured, and the rest flutter wildly off into the darkness.

Poachers often come to untimely ends. Here is an actual incident which befell one

of my companions—as clever a poacher, and
as decent and quiet a man as need be.   I saw
him on the night previous to the morning of
his death, though he did not see me.   It was
a night at the end of October.   The winds
had stripped the leaves from the trees, and
the dripping branches stood starkly against the
sky.   I was on the high road with a vehicle,
when plashes of rain began to descend, and a
low muttering came from out the dull leaden
clouds.   As the darkness increased, occasional
flashes tore zig-zag across the sky, and the rain
set to a dead pour.   The lightning only served
to increase the darkness.   I could just see the
mare's steaming shoulders butting away in
front, and her sensitive ears alternately pricked
out on the track.   The pitchy darkness increased, I gave the mare her head, and let the
reins hang loosely on her neck.   The lightning
was terrible, the thunder almost continuous,
when the mare came to a dead stop.   I got
down from the trap and found her trembling
violently, with perspiration pouring down
her flanks.   All her gear was white with

lather, and I thought it best to lead her on to where I knew was a chestnut tree, and there wait for a lull in the storm. As I stood waiting, a black lurcher slunk along under the sodden hedge, and seeing the trap, immediately stopped and turned in its tracks. Having warned its master, the two reconnoitered and then came on together. The "Otter" (for it was he), bade a gruff " good-night " to the enshrouded vehicle and passed on into the darkness. He slouched rapidly under the rain, and went in the direction of extensive woods and coverts. Hundreds of pheasants had taken to the tall trees, and, from beneath, were visible against the sky. Hares abounded on the fallows, and rabbits swarmed everywhere. The storm had driven the keepers to their cosy hearths, and the prospect was a poacher's paradise. Just what occurred next can only be surmised. Doubtless the "Otter" worked long and earnestly through that terrible night, and at dawn staggered from the ground under a heavy load.

G

Just at dawn the poacher's wife emerged from a poor cottage at the junction of the roads, and after looking about her as a hunted animal might look, made quietly off over the land.   Creeping closely by the fences she covered a couple of miles, and then entered a disused, barn-like building.   Soon she emerged under a heavy load, her basket, as of old, covered with crisp, green cresses   These she had kept from last evening, when she plucked them in readiness, from the spring.   After two or three journeys she had removed the " plant," and as she eyed the game her eyes glistened, and she waited now only for *him*.   As yet she knew not that he would never more come— that soon she would be a lone and heart-broken creature.   For, although his life was one long warfare against the Game Laws, he had always been good and kind to her.   His end had come as it almost inevitably must.   The sound of a heavy unknown footstep on his way home, had turned him from his path.   He had then made back for the lime-kiln to obtain warmth and to dry his sodden clothes.   Once on the margin he was soon asleep. The fumes dulled his senses, and in his restless sleep he had rolled on to the stones. In the morning the Limestone Burner coming to work found a handful of pure white ashes. A few articles were scattered about, and he guessed the rest.

And so the "Otter" went to God . . . . The storm cleared, and the heavens were calm. In the sky, on the air, in the blades of grass were signs of awakening life. Morning came bright and fair, birds flew hither and thither, and the autumn flowers stood out to the sun. All things were glad and free, but one wretched stricken thing.

Chapter 7.

SALMON AND TROUT POACHING.

Flashes the blood-red gleam
    Over the midnight slaughter ;
Wild shadows haunt the stream ;
    Dark forms glance o'er the water.
It is the leisterers' cry !
    A salmon, ho ! oho !
In scales of light, the creature bright
    Is glimmering below.

MOST country poachers begin by loving
Nature and end by hating the Game
Laws. Whilst many a man is
willing to recognize "property" in hares and

pheasants, there are few who will do so with regard to salmon and trout. And this is why fish poachers have always swarmed. A sea-salmon is in the domain of the whole world one day; in a trickling runner among the hills the next. Yesterday it belonged to anybody; and the poacher, rightly or wrongly, thinks it belongs to him if only he can snatch it. There are few fish poachers who in their time have not been anglers; and anglers are of two kinds : there are those who fish fair, and those who fish foul. The first set are phillosophical and cultivate patience: the second are preda-

tory and catch fish, fairly if they can—but they catch fish.

Just as redwings and field-fares constitute the first game of young gunners, so the loach, the minnow, and the stickleback, are the prey of the young poacher. If these things are small, they are by no means to be despised, for there is a tide in the affairs of men when these "small fry" of the waters afford as much sport on their pebbly shallows as do the silvery-sided salmon in the pools of Strathspay. As yet there is no knowledge of gaff or click hook—only of a willow wand, a bit of string, and a croocked pin. The average country urchin has always a considerable dash of the savage in his composition, and this first comes out in relation to fish rather than fowl. See him during summer as he wantons in the stream like a dace. Watch where his brown legs carry him ; observe his stealthy movements as he raises the likely stones ; and note the primitive poaching weapon in his hand. That old pronged fork is every whit as formidable to the loach and bullhead as is the lister of the man-

poacher to salmon and trout—and the wader
uses it almost as skillfully. He has a bottle on
the bank, and into this he pours the fish unhurt
which he captures with his hands. Examine his
aquarium, and hidden among the weeds you
will find three or four species of small fry.
The loach, the minnow, and the bullhead are
sure to be there, with perhaps a tiny stickleback, and somewhere, outside the bottle—
stuffed in cap or breeches pocket—crayfish of
every age and size. During a long life I have
watched the process, and this is the stuff out
of which fish-poachers are made.

It is part of the wisdom of nature's economy
that when furred and feathered game is "out,"
fish are "in." It might be thought that
poachers would recognize neither times nor
seasons, but this is a mistake. During fence
time game is nearly worthless; and then the
prospective penalties of poaching out of season
have to be taken into account. Fish poaching
is practised none the less for the high preserva-
tion and strict watching which so much prevails
now-a-days; it seems even to have grown

with them. In outlying country towns with
salmon and trout streams in the vicinity,
poaching is carried on to an almost incredible
extent. There are men who live by it and
women to whom it constitutes a thriving trade.
The "Otter," more thrifty than the rest of us,
has purchased a cottage with the proceeds of
his poaching ; and I know four or five families
who live by it. Whilst our class provide the
chief business of the country police courts, and
is a great source of profit to the local fish and
game dealer, there is quite another and a
pleasanter side, to the picture. But this later.
The wary poacher never starts for the fishing
ground without having first his customer; and
it is surprising with what lax code of morals
the provincial public will deal, when the silent
night worker is one to the bargain. Of course
the public always gets cheap fish and fresh fish,
so fresh indeed that sometimes the life has
hardly gone out of it. It is a perfectly easy
matter to provide fish and the only difficulty lies
in conveying it into the towns and villages. I
never knew but what I might be met by some

county constable, and consequently never carried game upon me. This I secreted in stack, rick, or disused farm building, until such time as it could be safely fetched. Country carriers, early morning milk-carts, and women are all employed in getting the hauls into town. In this women are by far the most successful. Sometimes they are seen labouring under a heavy load carried in a sack, with faggots and rotten sticks protruding from the mouth ; or again, with a large basket innocently covered with crisp, green cresses which effectually hide the bright silvery fish beneath. Our methods of fish poaching are many. As we work silently and in the night, the chances of success are all in our favour. We walk much by the stream side during the day, and take mental notes of men and fish. We know the beats of the watchers, and have the water-side by heart. Long use has accustomed us to work as well in the dark as in the light, and this is essential. During summer, when the water is low, the fish congregate in deep "dubs." This they do for protection, and

here, if overhung by trees, there is always
abundance of food.   Whenever it was our
intention to net a dub, we carefully examined
every inch of its bottom beforehand.   If it had
been "thorned," every thorn was carefully
removed — small thorn bushes with stones
attached, and thrown in by the watchers to
entangle nets.   Of course fish-poaching can
never be tackled single-handed.   In "long-
netting" the net is dragged by a man on each
side, a third wading after to lift it over the
stakes, and to prevent the fish from escaping.
When the end of the pool is reached the
salmon and trout are simply drawn out upon
the pebbles.   This is repeated through the
night until half-a-dozen pools are netted—
probably depopulated of their fish.   Netting
of this description is a wholesale method of
capture, always supposing that we are allowed
our own time.   It requires to be done slowly,
however, as if alarmed we can do nothing but
abandon the net.   This is necessarily large,
and when thoroughly wet is cumbersome
and exceedingly heavy.   The loss of one of

TICKLING TROUT.

our large nets was a serious matter, not only in time but money. For narrow streams, a narrow net is used, this being attached to two poles. It is better to cut the poles (of ash) only when required, as they are awkward objects to carry. The method of working the " pod-net " is the same in principle as the last. The older fish poachers rarely go in for poisoning. This is a cowardly method, and kills everything, both great and small, for miles down stream. Chloride of lime is the agent mostly used, as it does not injure the edible parts. The lime is thrown into the river where fish are known to lie, and its deadly influence is soon seen. The fish, weakened and poisoned, float belly uppermost. This at once renders them conspicuous, and they are simply lifted out of the water in a landing-net. Salmon and trout which come by their death in this way have the usually pink parts of a dull white, with the eyes and gill-covers of the same colour, and covered with a fine white film. This substance is much used in mills on the banks of trout-streams, and probably more fish are " poached " by this kind of pollution in a month than the most inveterate moucher will kill in a year.

It is only poachers of the old school that are careful to observe close times, and they do their work mostly in summer. Many of the younger and more desperate hands, however, do really serious business when the fish are out of season. When salmon and trout are spawning their senses seem to become dulled, and then they are not difficult to approach in the water. They seek the highest reaches to spawn and stay for a considerable time on the spawning beds. A salmon offers a fair mark, and these are obtained by spearing. The pronged salmon spear is driven into the fleshy shoulders of the fish, when it is hauled out on to the bank. In this way I have often killed more fish in a single day than I could possibly carry home—even when there was little or no chance of detection. There is only one practicable way of carrying a big salmon across country on a dark night, and that is by hanging it round one's neck and steadying it in front. I have left tons of fish behind when chased by the watchers, as of all

things they are the most difficult to carry. The best water bailiffs are those who are least seen, or who watch from a distance. So as to save sudden surprise, and to give timely warning of the approach of watchers, one of the poaching party should always coammnd the land from a tree top.

The flesh of spawning fish is loose and watery, insipid and tasteless, and rarely brings more than a few pence per pound. In an out-lying hamlet known to me, poached salmon, during last close time, was so common that the cottagers fed their poultry upon it through the winter. Several fish were killed each over 20 lbs. in weight. Than netting, another way of securing salmon and trout from the spawning redds is by "click" hooks. These are simply large salmon hooks bound shaft to shaft and attached to a long cord ; a bit of lead balances them and adds weight. These are used in the "dubs" when spearing by wading is impracticable. When a salmon is seen the hooks are simply thrown beyond it, then gently dragged until they come immediately beneath ; when a

H

sharp click sends them into the soft under
parts of the fish, which is then dragged out.
As the pike, which is one of nature's poachers,
is injurious to our interests as well as those of
the angler, we never miss an opportunity of
treating him in the same summary manner.
Of course, poaching with click-hooks requires
to be done during the day, or by the aid of an
artificial light.   Light attracts salmon just as it
attracts birds, and tar brands are frequently
used by poachers.   A good, rough bulls-eye
lantern, to aid in spearing, can be made
from a disused salmon canister.   A circular
hole should be made in the side, and a bit of
material tied over to hide the light when not in
use.   Shooting is sometimes resorted to, but
for this class of poaching the habits and beats
of the water bailiffs require to be accurately
known.   The method has the advantage of
quickness, and a gun in skilful hands and at
short distance may be used without injuring
the fleshy parts of the fish.   That deadly bait,
salmon row, is now rarely used, the method of
preparing it being unknown to the younger

generation. It can, however, be used with deadly effect. Although both ourselves and our nets were occasionally captured, the watchers generally found this a difficult matter. In approaching our fishing grounds we did not mind going sinuously and snake - like

through the wet meadows, and as I have said, our nets were rarely kept at home. These were secreted in stone heaps, and among bushes in close proximity to where we intended to use them. Were they kept at home the obtaining of a search warrant by the police or local

H 2

Angling Association would always render their
custody a critical business.   When, upon any
rare occasion, the nets were kept at home, it was
only for a short period, and when about to be
used.   Sometimes, though rarely, the police
have discovered them secreted in the chimney,
between bed and mattrass, or, in one case,
wound about the portly person of a poacher's
wife.   As I have already said, the women are
not always simply aiders and abettors, but
in the actual poaching sometimes play an
important part.   They have frequently been
taken red-handed by the watchers.   Mention of
the water-bailiffs reminds me that I must say a
word of them too.   Their profession is a hard
one—harder by far than the poacher's.   They
work at night, and require to be most on the
alert during rough and wet weather; especially
in winter when fish are spawning.   Sometimes they must remain still for hours in
freezing clothes; and even in summer not
unfrequently lie all night in dank and wet
herbage.   They see the night side of nature,
and many of them are as good naturalists as

the poachers. If a lapwing gets up and screams in the darkness the cleverer of them know how to interpret the sound, as also a hare rushing wildly past. I must add, however, that it is in the nature of things that at all points the fish poacher is cleverer and of readier wit than the river watcher.

Looking back it does not seem long since county constables first became an institution in this part of the country. I remember an amusing incident connected with one of them who was evidently a stranger to many of the phases of woodcraft. We

had been netting a deep dub just below a stone bridge, and were about to land a splendid haul.

Looking up, a constable was watching our operations in an interested sort of way, and for a moment we thought we were fairly caught. Just as we were about to abandon the net and make off through the wood, the man spoke. In an instant I saw how matters stood. He failed to grasp the situation—even came down and helped us to draw the net on to the bank. In thanking us for a silvery five-pound salmon we gave him he spoke with a southern accent, and I suppose that poachers and poaching were subjects that had never entered into his philosophy.

Chapter 8.

GROUSE POACHING.

FOR pleasurable excitement, to say nothing of profit, the pick of all poaching is for grouse. However fascinating partridge poaching may be ; however pleasurable picking off pheasants from bare boughs ; or the night-piercing screams of a netted hare —none of these can compare with the wild work of the moors. I am abroad on the heather just before the coming of the day. My way lies now along the rugged course of a fell "beck," now along the lower shoulder of the mountain. The grey dissolves into dawn, the dawn into light, and the first blackcock crows to his grey hen in the hollow. As my head appears above the burn side, the ever-watchful curlews whistle and the plovers scream. A dotterel goes plaintively piping over the stones, and the "cheep, cheep," of the awakening ling-birds rises from every brae. A silent tarn lies shimmering in a green hollow beneath, and over its marge constantly flit a pair of summer snipe. The bellowing of red deer comes from a neighbouring corrie, and a herd of roe are browsing on the confines of the scrub. The sun mounts the Eastern air, drives the mists away and beyond the lichen patches loved by the ptarmigan—and it is day.

.A glorious bird is the red grouse ! Listen to his warning "kok, kok, kok," as he eyes the invader of his moorland haunts. Now that it is day his mate joins him on the "knowe." The sun warms up his rufus plumage, and the crescent-shaped patch of vermilion over the eye glows in the strong light. It is these

sights and sounds that warm me to my work,
and dearly I love the moor-game. Years ago
I had sown grain along the fell-side so as to
entice the grouse within range of an old flint-
lock which I used with deadly effect from
behind a stone wall. Then snares were set on
the barley sheaves and corn stooks, by which a
brace of birds were occasionally bagged. In
after years an unforseen grouse harvest came
in quite an unexpected manner. With the
enclosure of the Commons hundreds of miles of
wire fencing was erected, and in this way,
before the birds had become accustomed to it,
numbers were killed by flying against the

fences. The casualties mostly occurred during
"thick" weather, or when the mists had
clung to the hills for days. At such times
grouse fly low, and strike before seeing the
obstacle. I never failed to note the mist-
caps hanging to the fell-tops, and then, bag in
hand, walked parallel to miles and miles of
flimsy fence. Sometimes a dozen brace of
birds were picked up in a morning; and, on the
lower grounds, an occasional partridge, woodcock, or snipe.

Grouse are the only game that ever tempted
me to poach during close time, and then I only
erred by a few days. Birds sold in London on
the morning of the "Twelfth" bring the big-
gest prices of the season, and to supply the
demand was a temptation I could never resist.
Many a "Squire," many a Country Justice
has been tempted as I was, and fell as I fell.
It is not too much to say that every one of the
three thousand birds sold in London on the
opening day has been poached during the
"fence" time. In the north, country station-
masters find hampers dropped on their plat-

forms addressed to London dealers, but, as to who brought them, or how they came there, none ever knows.

The only true prophet of the grouse-moors is the poacher. Months before the "squire" and keeper he knows whether disease will assert itself or no. By reason of his out-door life he has accuracy of eye and judgment sufficient to interpret what he sees aright. He is abroad in all weathers, and through every hour of the day and night. His clothes have taken on them the duns and browns of the moorlands; and he owns the subtle influence which attracts wild creatures to him. He has watched grouse "at home" since the beginning of the year. On the first spring day the sun shines brightly at noon. The birds bask on the brae, and spread their wings to the warmth. As the sun gains in power, and spring comes slowly up the way, the red grouse give out gurgling notes, and indulge in much strutting. The fell "becks" sparkles in the sun; the merlin screams over the heather, and the grouse packs break up.

The birds are now seen singly or in pairs, and brae answers brae from dawn till dark. The cock grouse takes his stand on some grey rock, and erects or depresses at pleasure his ver- milion eye-streak. Pairing is not long con- tinued, and the two find out a depression in the heather which they line with bents and mountain grasses. About eight eggs are laid, and the cock grouse takes his stand upon the "knowe" to guard the nest from predaceous carrion and hooded crows. If hatching is successful the young birds are quickly on their legs, and through spring and summer follow the brooding birds. They grow larger and plumper each day, until it is difficut to detect them from the adult. Meanwhile August has come, and soon devastating death is dealt out to them. The sport, so far as the poacher is concerned, begins at the first rolling away of the morning mists ; and then he often makes the best bag of the year. It was rarely that I was abroad later than two in the morning, and my first business was to wade out thigh-deep into the purple heather. From such a position it is not difficult to locate the crowing of the moorbirds as they answer each other across the heather. When this was done I would gain a rough stone wall, and then, by imitating the gurgling call-notes of cock or hen I could bring up every grouse within hearing. Sometimes a dozen would be about me at one time. Then the birds were picked off as they flew over the knolls and braes, or as they boldly stood on any eminence near. If this method is deadly in early August, it is infinitely more so during pairing time. Then, if time and leisure be allowed, and the poacher is a good " caller," almost every bird on a moor may be bagged.

The greatest number of grouse, and consequently the best poaching, is to be had on moors on which the heather is regularly burned. Grouse love the shoots of ling which spring up after burning, and the birds which feed upon this invariably have the brightest plumage. On a well-burnt moor the best poaching method is by using a silk net. By watching for traces during the day it is not difficult to detect

where the birds roost, and once this is discovered the rest is easy. The net is trailed
along the ground by two men, and dropped in-
stantly on the whirr of wings. The springing
of the birds is the only guide in the darkness,
though the method skilfully carried out is most
destructive, and sometimes a whole covey is
is bagged at one sweep. Silk nets have three
good qualities for night work, those made of
any other material being cumbersome and
nearly useless. They are light, strong, and
are easily carried. It is well to have about
eighteen inches of glazed material along the
bottom of the net, or it is apt to catch in
dragging. Where poaching is practised, keepers
often place in the likeliest places a number of
strong stakes armed with protruding nails.
These, however, may be removed and re-
planted after the night's work; or, just at dusk
a bunch of white feathers may be tied to point
the position of each.

The planting of grain patches along the
moor-side has been mentioned, and on these in
late autumn great numbers of birds are bagged.

Grouse are exceedingly fond of oats, and in the early morning the stooks are sometimes almost black with them. A pot shot here from behind a wall or fence is generally a profitable one, as the heavy charge of shot is sent straight at the " brown." Black-game are as keen as red grouse on oats, and a few sheaves thrown about always attracts them. Although the blackcock is a noble bird in appearance, he is dull and heavy, and is easily bagged. Early in the season the birds lie until almost trod upon, and of all game are the easiest to net. They roost on the ground, and usually seek out some sheltered brae-side on which to sleep. If closely watched at evening, it is not difficult to clap a silk net over them upon the first favourable night, when both mother and grown young are bagged together. That there are gentlemen poachers as well as casuals and amateurs, the following incident relating to black-game shows : "On a dull misty day they are easily got at : they will sit on the thorn bushes and alders, and let the shooter pick them off

one by one.   I remember once, on such a day,
taking a noble sportsman who was very keen
to shoot a blackcock, up to some black game
sitting on a thorn hedge.   When he got within
about twenty-five yards he fired his first barrel
(after taking a very deliberate aim) at an old
grey hen.   She took no notice, only shaking
her feathers a little, and hopping a short distance further on.   The same result with the
second barrel.   He loaded again and fired.
This time the old hen turned round, and
looked to see where the noise and unpleasant
tickling sensation came from, and grew un-
easy ; the next attempt made her fly on to where
her companions were sitting, and our friend
then gave up his weapon to me in despair.
Black game grow very stupid also when on
stubbles ; they will let a man fire at them, and
if they do not see him, will fly round the field
and settle again, or pitch on a wall quite near
to him.   Grouse will do the same thing.
There is not much 'sport' in such shooting
as this, but when out alone, and wanting to
make a bag, it is a sure and quick way to do

so. It may be called ' poaching '—all I can say is, there would be many more gentlemen poachers if they could obtain such chances, and could not get game in any other way."

Both grouse and black game may frequently be brought within range by placing a dead or stuffed bird on a rock or a stone wall. A small forked stick is made to support the head and neck of the decoy " dummy," which, if there are birds in the vicinity, soon attracts them. As a rule the lure is not long successful, but sufficiently so as to enable the poacher to make a big bag. Upon one occasion I made a remarkable addition to our fur and feather. In the darkness a movement was heard among the dense branches of a Scotch fir, when, looking up, a large bird which seemed as big as a turkey commenced to flutter off. It was stopped before it had flown many yards, and proved to be a handsome cock Capercailzie in splendid plumage. Had I been certain as to what it was I certainly should not have fired.

Grouse stalking is fascinating sport, and by this method I usually made my greatest achievements. The stalking was mainly done from behind an old moorland horse, with which I had struck up an acquaintance ; and it learned to stand fire like a war veteran. I used to think it enjoyed the sport, and I believe it did. With the aid of my shaggy friend I have successfully stalked hundreds of grouse, as its presence seemed to allay both fear and suspicion. Firing over its back, its neck, or beneath its belly—all were taken alike, patiently and sedately. An occasional handful of oats, or half a loaf, cemented the friendship of the old horse—my best and most constant poaching companion for years.

Rabbit Poaching.

IF well trained lurchers are absolutely necessary to hare poaching, ferrets are just as important to successful rabbit poaching. Nearly nothing in fur can be done without them. However lucky the moucher may be among pheasants, partridge, or grouse, rabbits are and must be the chief product of his nights. Of the methods of obtaining them—field netting, well-traps, shooting—all are as nothing compared with silent ferreting.

In the north we have two well-defined varieties of ferret—one a brown colour and

known as the polecat-ferret; the other, the
common white variety. The first is the hardier,
and it is to secure this quality that poachers
cross their ferrets with the wild polecat. Unlike
lurchers, ferrets require but little training, and
seem to work instinctively. There are various
reasons why poachers prefer white ferrets
to the polecat variety. At night a brown
ferret is apt to be nipped up in mistake for a
rabbit; while a white one is always apparent,
even when moving among the densest herbage.
Hence mouchers invariably use white ones.
Gamekeepers who know their business prefer
ferrets taken from poachers to any other. I
was always particularly careful in selecting
my stock, as from the nature of my trade I
could ill afford to use bad ones. Certain
strains of ferrets cause rabbits to bolt rapidly,
while others are slow and sluggish. It need
hardly be said that I always used the former.
Even the best, however, will sometimes drive
a rabbit to the end of a "blind" burrow; an
after killing it will not return until it ha
gorged itself with blood. And more troub

is added if the ferret curls itself up for an after-dinner sleep. Then it has either to be left or dug out. The latter process is long, the burrows ramify far into the mound, and it is not just known in which the ferret remains. If it be left it is well to bar every hole with stones, and then return with a dead rabbit when hunger succeeds the gorged sleep. It is to guard against such occasions as these that working ferrets are generally muzzled. A cruel practise used to obtain among poachers of stitching together the lips of ferrets to prevent their worrying rabbits and then "laying up." For myself I made a muzzle of soft string which was effective, and at the same time comfortable to wear. When there was a chance of being surprised at night work I occasionally worked ferrets with a line attached ; but this is an objectionable practice and does not always answer. There may be a root or stick in which the line gets entangled, when there will be digging and no end of trouble to get the ferret out. From these facts, and the great uncertainty of ferreting, it will be understood why poachers

can afford to use only the best animals. A
tangled hedgebank with coarse herbage was
alwasy a favourite spot for my depredations.
There are invariably two, often half a dozen
holes, to the same burrow. Small purse nets
are spread over these, and I always preferred
these loose to being pegged or fixed in any
way. When all the nets are set the ferrets are
turned in. They do not proceed immediately,
but sniff the mouth of the hole ; their inde-
cision is only momentary, however, for soon
the tip of the tail disappears in the darkness.
And now silence is essential to success, as
rabbits refuse to bolt if there is the slightest
noise outside. A dull thud, a rush, and a
rabbit goes rolling over and over entangled in
the purse. Reserve nets are quickly clapped on
the holes as the rabbits bolt, the latter invariably being taken except where a couple come
together. Standing on the mound a shot would
stop these as they go bounding through the
dead leaves, but the sound would bring up the
keeper, and so one has to practise self-denial.
Unlike hares, rabbits rarely squeal when they

become entangled; and this allows one to ferret long and silently. Rabbits bolt best on a windy day and before noon; after that they are sluggish and often refuse to come out at all. This is day ferreting, but of course mine was done mainly at night. In this case the dogs always ranged the land, and drove everything off it before we commenced operations. On good ground a mound or brae sometimes seemed to explode with rabbits, so wildly did they fly before their deadly foe. I have seen a score driven from one set of holes, while five or six couples is not at all uncommon. When ferrets are running the burrows, stoats and weasels are occasionally driven out; and among other strange things unearthed I remember a brown owl, a stock-dove, and a shell-drake— each of which happened to be breeding in the mounds.

The confines of a large estate constitute a poacher's paradise, for although partridge and grouse require land suited to their taste, rabbits and pheasants are common to all preserved ground. And then the former may be taken at any time, and in so many different ways. They are abundant, too, and always find a ready market. The penalties attached to rabbit poaching are less than those of game, and the conies need not be followed into closely preserved coverts. The extermination of the rabbit will be contemporaneous with that of the lurcher and poacher—two institutions of village life which date back to the time of the New Forest. Of the many mouching modes for taking conies, ferretting, as already stated, and field netting are the most common. Traps with steel jaws are sometimes set in runs, inserted in the turf so as to bring them flush with the sward. But destruction by this method is not sufficiently wholesale, and the upturned white under-parts of the rabbit's fur show too plainly against the green. The poacher's methods must be quick, and he cannot afford to visit by day traps set in the dark. The night must cover all his doings. When the unscrupulous keeper finds a snare he sometimes puts a leveret into it, and secretes himself. Then he waits, and captures the poacher "in the act." As with some other methods already mentioned, the trap poacher is only a casual. Ferretting is silent and almost invariably successful. In warrens, both inequalities of the ground, mounds, and ditches af- ford good cover. My best and most wholesale

method of field-poaching for rabbits was by means of two long nets. These are from a hun- dred to a hundred and fifty yards in length, and about four feet high. They are usually made of silk, and are light and strong, and easily portable. These are set parallel to each other along the edge of a wood, about thirty yards out into the pasture. Only about four inches divides the nets. A dark windy night is best for the work, as in such weather rabbits feed far out in the fields. On a night of this character, too, the game neither hears nor sees the poacher. The nets are long—the first small in mesh, that immediately behind large. When a rabbit or hare strikes, the impetus takes a part of the first net and its contents through the larger mesh of the second, and there, hanging, the creature struggles until it is knocked on the head with a stick. Immediately the nets are set, two men and a brace of lurchers range the ground in front, slowly and patiently, and gradually drive every feeding thing woodwards. A third man quietly paces the sward behind the nets, killing whatever strikes them. In this way I have taken many scores of rabbits in a single night. On the confines of a large estate a rather clever trick was once played upon us. Each year about half-a-dozen black or white rabbits were turned down into certain woods. Whilst feeding, these stood out conspicuously from the rest, and were religiously preserved. Upon these the keepers kept a close watch, and when any were missing it was suspected what was going on, when the watching strength was increased. As soon as we detected the trick, we were careful to let the coloured rabbits go free. We found that it was altogether to our interest to preserve them.

During night poaching for rabbits and hares the ground game is driven from its feeding ground to the woods or copses. Precisely the reverse method is employed during the day when the game is in cover. The practice is to find a spinny in which both rabbits and hares are known to lie ; and then to set purse nets on the outside of every opening which may possibly be used by the frightened animals. The smaller the wood or patch of cover the easier it is to work. A man, with or without a dog, enters the covert, and his presence soon induces the furry denizens to bolt. As these rush through their customary runs they find themselves in the meshes of a net, and every struggle only makes them faster. This method has the disadvantage of being done in the light, but where there is much game is very deadly.

Snares for hares and rabbits are not used nearly so much now as formerly. For all that, they are useful in outlying districts, or on land that is not closely watched. For hares the snare is a wire noose tied to a stick with string, and placed edgeways in the trod. To have the snare the right height is an important matter ; and it will be found that two fists high for a hare, and one for a rabbit, is the most deadly. Casuals set their snares in hedge-bottoms, but these are no good. Two òr three feet away from the hedge is the most killing position —for this reason : when a hare canters up to a fence it never immediately bounds through ; it pauses about a yard away, then leaps into the hedge-bottom. It is during this last leap that it puts its neck into the noose and is taken. If a keeper merely watches a snare until it is "lifted," good and well ; but to put a hare or rabbit into it and then pounce on the moucher—well, that is a different matter. It is not difficult to see where a hare has been taken, especially if the run in which the snare was set was damp. There will be the hole where the peg has been, and the ground will be beaten flat by the struggles of the animal in endeavouring to free itself.

Field-netting for rabbits may be prevented in the same way as for partridges—by thorning the ground where the game feeds. It is quite a mistake to plant thorns, or even to stake out large branches. The only ones that at all trouble the poacher are small thorns which are left absolutely free on the ground. These get into the net, roll it up hopelessly in a short time, and if this once occurs everything escapes. Large thorns are easily seen and easily removed, but the abominable ones are the small ones left loose on the surface of the ground.

The most certain and wholesale method of rabbit poaching I ever practised was also the most daring. The engine employed was the "well-trap." This is a square, deep box, built into the ground, and immediately opposite to a smoot-hole in the fence through which the rabbits run from wood or covert to field or pasture. Through a hole in the wall or fence a wooden trough or box is inserted. As the rabbits run through, the floor opens beneath their weight, and they drop into the "well." Immediately the pressure is removed the floor springs back to its original position, and thus a score or more rabbits are often taken in a single night. In the construction of these "well-traps," rough and unbarked wood is used, though, even after this precaution, the rabbits will not take them for weeks. Then, they become familiar; the weather washes away all scent, and the "well" is a wholesale engine of destruction. All surface traces of the existence of the trap must be covered over with dead leaves and woodland debris. The rabbits, of course, are taken alive, and the best way of killing them is by stretching them across the knee, and so dislocating the spine. If the keeper once finds out the trap the game is up. Whilst it lasts, however, it kills more rabbits than every other stroke of woodcraft the poacher knows.

Chapter 10.

Tricks.

*W*HEN it is known that a man's life is one long protest against the Game Laws he has to be exceedingly careful of his comings and goings. Every constable, every gamekeeper, and most workers in woodcraft are aware of the motives which bring him abroad at night. More eyes are upon him than he sees, and no one knows better than he that the enemies most to be feared are those who are least seen ; and the man who has tasted the bitterness of poaching penalties will do everything in his power to escape detection.   Probably the greatest aid to this end is knowing the country by heart ; the field-paths and disused bye-ways, the fordable parts of the river, and a hundred things beside.   The poacher is and must be suspicious of everyone he meets.

In planning and carrying out forays I was always careful to observe two conditions.   No poaching secret was ever confided to another ; and I invariably endeavoured to get to the ground unseen.   If my out-going was observed it often entailed a circuit of a dozen miles in coming home, and even then the entry into town was not without considerable risk.   The hand of everyone was against me in my unlawful calling, and many were the shifts I had to make to escape detection or capture. To show with what success this may be carried out, the following incident will show.

I conceived the idea of openly shooting certain well-stocked coverts during the temporary absence of the owner. These were so well watched that all the ordinary measures at night seemed likely to be baffled. To openly shoot during broad day, and under the very eye of the keeper, was now the essential part of the programme ; and to this end I must explain as follows : The keeper on the estate was but lately come to the district. Upon two occasions when I had been placed in the dock, I had been described as " a poacher of gentlemanly appearance, ' and " the gentleman poacher again." (My forefathers had been small estatesmen for generations, and I suppose that some last lingering air of gentility attached to me). Well, I had arranged with a confederate to act as bag carrier ; he was to be very servile, and not to forget to touch his cap at pretty frequent intervals. After " making up " as a country squire—(I had closely studied the species on the "Bench,")— and providing a luncheon in keeping with my temporary " squiredom," we started for the

K 2

woods. It was a bright morning in the last
week of October, and game—hares, pheasants,
and woodcock—was exceedingly plentiful.
The first firing brought up the keeper, who
touched his hat in the most respectful fashion.
He behaved, in short, precisely as I would
have had him behave. I lost no time on
quietly congratulating him on the number and
quality of his birds; told him that his master
would return from town to-morrow (which
I had learned incidentally), and ended by
handing him my cartridge bag to carry. A
splendid bag of birds had been made by luncheon time, and the viands which constituted
the meal were very much in keeping with my
assumed position. Dusk came at the close of
the short October afternoon, and with it the
end of our day's sport. The bag was spread
out in one of the rides of the wood, and in
imagination I can see it now—thirty-seven
pheasants, nine hares, five woodcock, a few
rabbits, some cushats, and the usual " miscel-
laneous." The man of gaiters was despatched
a couple of miles for a cart to carry the spoil,

and a substantial " tip " gave speed to his not
unwilling legs. The game, however, was not
to occupy the cart. A donkey with panniers

was waiting in a clump of brush by the covert
side, and as soon as the panniers were packed,
its head was turned homeward over a wild bit
of moorland. With the start obtained, chase
would have been fruitless had it ever been
contemplated—which it never was. I need
not detail the sequel to the incident here, and

may say that it was somewhat painful to myself as well as my bag carrier. And I am sorry to say that the keeper was summarily dismissed by the enraged squire as a reward for his innocence. As to the coverts, they were so well stocked, that after a few days' rest there appeared as much game as ever, and the contents of our little bag were hardly missed.

Another trick to which my co-worker used to resort was to attire himself in broad-brimmed hat and black coat similar to those worn a century ago by the people called Quakers. In the former he carried his nets, and in the capacious pockets of the latter the game he took. These outward guarantees of good faith, away from his own parish, precluded him from ever once being searched. I have already remarked, and every practical poacher knows it to be the fact, that the difficulty is not so much to obtain game as to transport it safely home. Although our dogs were trained to run on a hundred yards in advance so as to give warning of the approach of a possible enemy—even this did not always save us. A big bag of game handicaps one severely in a cross-country run, and it is doubly galling to have to sacrifice it. Well, upon the particular occasion to which I refer there was to be a country funeral with a hearse from the neighbouring market town, and of this I was determined to take advantage. By arranging with the driver I was enabled to stow myself and a large haul in the body of the vehicle, and, although the journey was a cramped and stuffy one, we in time reached our destination. As we came behind the nearest game shop the driver undid the door, and the questionable corpse was safely landed.

I need hardly say that in a long life of poaching there were many occasions when I was brought to book. These, however, would form but a small percentage of the times I was " out." My success in this way was probably owing to the fact that I was chary as to those I took into confidence, and knew that above all things keeping my own council was the best wisdom. Another moucher I knew, but with whom I would have nothing to do, was an instance of one who told poaching secrets to village gossips. The " Mole " spent most of *his* time in the county gaol, and just lately he completed his sixty-fifth incarceration —only a few of which were for offences outside the game laws. Well, there came a time when all the keepers round the country side had their revenge on me, and they made the most of it. I and my companion were fairly caught by being driven into an ambuscade by a combination of keepers. Exultant in my capture, the keepers from almost every estate in the neighbourhood flocked to witness my conviction. Some of them who had at times only seen a vanishing form in the darkness, now attended to see the man, as they put it. As I had always been followed at nights by an old black bitch, she, too, was produced in court, and proved an object of much curiosity. Well,

our case was called, and, as we had no good
defence to set up, it was agreed that my companion should do the talking. Without letting
it appear so, we had a very definite object in
prolonging the hearing of the case. There was
never any great inclination to hurry such
matters, as the magistrates always seemed to
enjoy them. "We had been taken in the act,"
my co-worker told the bench. "We deserved
no quarter, and asked none. Poaching was
right by the Bible, but wrong by the law,"—

and so he was rushing on. One of the Justices
deigned to remark that it was a question of
"property" not morality. "Oh!" rejoined
the "Otter," "because blue blood doesn't run

in my veins that's no reason why I shouldn't
have my share. But its a queer kind of
property that's yours in that field, mine on the
turnpike, and a third man's over the next
fence." The end of it was, however, a fine of
£5, with an alternative. And so the case
ended. But that day the keepers and their
assistants had forgotten the first principles of
watching. The best keeper is the one that is
the least seen. Only let the poacher know his
whereabouts, and the latter's work is easy. It
was afterwards remarked that during our trial
not a poacher was in court. To any keeper
skilled in his craft this fact must have appeared
unusual—and significant. It became even more
so when both of us were released by reason of
our heavy fine having been paid the same
evening. Most of the keepers had had their
day out, and were making the most of it.
Had their heads not been muddled they might
have seen more than one woman labouring
under loaded baskets near the local game
dealers ; these innocently covered with mantling cresses, and so, at the time, escaping

suspicion. Upon the memorable day the
pheasants had been fed by unseen hands—and
had vanished. The only traces left by the
covert side were fluffy feathers everywhere.
Few hares remained on the land ; the rest had
either been snared or netted at the gates. The
rabbits' burrows had been ferreted, the ferrets
having been slyly borrowed at the keeper's
cottage during his absence for the occasion. I
may say that, in connection with this incident,
we always claimed to poach square, and drew
the line at home-reared pheasants—allowing
them "property." Those found wild in the
woods were on a different footing, and we directed our whole knowledge of woodcraft
against them.

Here is another "court" incident, in which
I and my companion played a part. We came
in contact with the law just sufficient to make
us know something of its bearings. When
charged with being in possession of "game"
we reiterated the old argument that rabbits
were vermin—but it rarely stood us in good
stead. On one occasion, however, we scored.

Being committed for two months for " night
poaching," we respectfully informed the presiding Justice that, at the time of our capture,
the sun had risen an hour ; and further, that
the law did not allow more than half the sentence just passed upon us. Our magistrate
friend—to whom I have more than once re-
ferred—was on the bench, and he told his
brother Justices that he thought there was
something in the contention. The old Clerk
looked crabbed as he fumbled for his horn
spectacles, and, after turning over a book
called " Stone's Justices' Manual," he solemnly
informed the bench that defendants in their
interpretation were right. We naturally remember this little incident, and as the law has
had the whip hand of us upon so many occasions, chuckle over it.

We invariably made friends with the stone-
breakers by the road-sides, and just as invariably carried about us stone-breakers'
hammers, and " preserves " for the eyes.
When hard pressed, and if unknown to the
pursuing keeper, nothing is easier than to dis-

miss the dog, throw off one's coat, plump
down upon the first stone heap on the road,
and go to work. If the thing is neatly done,
and the " preserves " cover the face, it is
wonderful how often this ruse is successful.
The keeper may put a hasty question, but he
oftener rushes after his man. Mention of
stone-heaps reminds me of the fact that they
are better " hides " for nets than almost any-
thing else, especially the larger unbroken
heaps. We invariably hid our big cumbrous
fishing nets beneath them, and the stones
were just as invariably true to their trust.

Going back to my earliest poaching days I
remember a cruel incident which had a very
different ending to what its author intended.
A young keeper had made a wager that he
would effect my capture within a certain number of days, and my first intimation of this
fact was a sickening sight which I discovered
in passing down a woodland glade just at dawn
on a bright December morning. I heard a
groan, and a few yards in front saw a man
stretched across the ride. His clothes were

covered with hoar frost, he was drenched in blood, and the poor fellow's pale face showed me that of the keeper. He was held fast in a man-trap which had terribly lacerated his lower limbs. He was conscious, but quite exhausted. Although in great agony he suffered me to carry him to a neighbouring hayrick, from whence we removed him to his cottage. He recovered slowly, and the mantrap which he had set the night before was, I believe, the last ever used in that district.

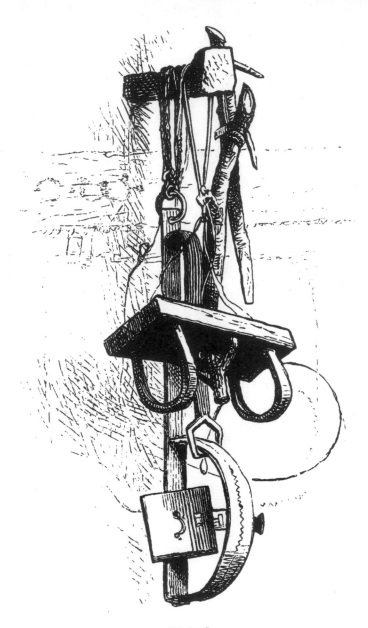

TRAPS.

Chapter 11.

PERSONAL ENCOUNTERS.

WHEN I had finished the last chapter I thought I had completed my work, but the gentleman who is to edit these "Confessions" now tells me that I am to confess more. He reminds me that I cannot have been an active poacher nearly all my life without having had numerous personal

encounters with keepers and others.   And in
this he is right.   But there is some difficulty in
my additional task for the following reasons :
I have never cared to take much credit to
myself for having broken the head of a keeper,
and there is but little pleasure to me in re-
counting the occasions when keepers have
broken mine.   However, speaking of broken
heads reminds me of an incident which was
amusing, though, at the time, somewhat painful to me.

One night in November when the trees were
bare, and the pheasants had taken to the
branches, we were in a mixed wood of pine
and beech.   A good many birds roosted on
its confines, and, to a practised eye, were not
difficult to see against the moon as they
sat on the lower limbs of the trees, near the
trunks.   I and my companion had old, strong
guns with barrels filed down, and, as we
got very near to the birds, we were using
small charges of powder.   As the night was
windy the shots would not be heard very far,
and we felt fairly safe.   When we had obtained

about three brace of birds, however, I heard a sudden crash among the underwood, when I immediately jumped behind the bole of a tree, and kept closely against it.

The head-keeper had my companion down before he could resist, and I only remained undiscovered for a few seconds. One of the under-keepers seized me, but, being a good wrestler, I soon threw him into a dense brake of brambles and blackthorn. Then I bolted with the third man close behind. I could easily have outrun him over the rough country that lay outside the wood, but—ah! these "buts"—there was a stiff stone fence fully five feet high betwixt me and the open. Unless I could "fly" the fence he would have me. I clutched my pockets, steadied myself for the leap—and then sprang. I heard my pursuer stop for a second to await the issue. Weighted as I was I caught the coping, and fell back heavily into the wood. As soon as the keeper saw I was down he rushed forward and hit me heavily on the head with a stave. The sharp corner cut right through the skin,

L 2

and blood spurted out in little jets. Then I
turned about, determined to close with my
opponent if he was inclined for further rough-
ness. But he was not. When he saw that
the blood was almost blinding me he dropped
his hedge-stake, and ran, apparently terrified
at what he had done. I leaned for a few
moments against the wall, then dragged myself
over, and started for a stream which ran down
the field. But I felt weaker at every step, and
soon crept into a bed of tall brackens, and
plugged the wound in my head with a handful
of wet moss, keeping it in position with my
neckerchief. After this I munched some
bread and hard cheese, sucked the dew from
the fern fronds, and then fell into a broken
sleep. I must have slept for four or five
hours, when I woke thirsty and feverish, and
very weak. I tried to walk, but again and
again fell down. Then I crawled for about a
hundred yards, but this caused my wound to
bleed afresh, and I fainted. Just as day was
coming a farm labourer came across, and
kindly helped me to his cottage. He and his

wife bathed my head and eyes, and then assisted me to the bed from which they had just risen. At noon I was able to take some bread and milk, and at night, an hour after darkness had fallen, I was able to start for home.

Well, the sequel came in due time. We each received a summons (my companion had been released after identification), we were tried in about a fortnight from the date of our capture. There was a full bench of Magistrates ; my companion pleaded guilty (with a view to a lenient sentence) ; myself—not guilty. In the first instance the case was clear, but not one of the three keepers (to their credit) would swear to me. They looked me carefully over, particularly my assailant. He was reminded that it was a fine, moonlight night. Yes, but his man, he thought, was taller, was more strongly built, and looked pale and haggard—no, he would not say that I was the man—in short, he thought I was not. Then came my innings. The keeper had sworn that, after running a mile, the poacher he chased had turned on him, and threatened to "do for him," if he advanced ;

that he had hit him on the head with his stick, and must have wounded him severely. He was also careful to explain that he had done this in " self defence." I then pointed out to the " bench " that it was no longer a matter of opinion ; that I claimed to have my head examined, and asked that the Police Superintendent, who was conducting the case, should settle the point.

But my assumption of an air of injured innocence had already done its work, and the presiding Magistrate said there was no evidence against me ; that the case as against me was dismissed.

I had hard work to get out of the box without smiling, for even then the pain in my head was acute, and I was not right for weeks after. I knew, however, that my wound was a dangerous possession, and close attention to my thick, soft hair, enabled me to hide it, always providing that it was not too closely examined. My companion was less fortunate, and his share of the proceedings, poor fellow, was " two months."

Here is the record of another encounter. There was a certain wood, the timber in which had been felled and carted. It had previously contained a good deal of " coppice," and after the wood-cutters had done their work, this had been utilized by the charcoal burners. The ashes from the charcoal had promoted quite an unseasonable growth, and everywhere about the stoles of the ash roots and hazel snags, fresh green grass and clover were springing. The hares on the neighbouring estate had found out this, and came nightly to the clearing to feed. As there were neither gaps nor gates we found it impossible to net them, and so had to resort to another device. Before the wood had been cleared rabbits had swarmed in it, and these had found ingress and egress through "smoots" in the stone fences. Upon examination we found that the larger of these were regularly used by our quarry, and, as we could not net them, we determined to plant a purse net at every smoot, drive the wood with fast dogs, and so bag our game. When everything was ready the lurchers

commenced their work, and, thoroughly
grasping the programme, worked up to it
admirably. Each dog that "found" drove its
hare fast and furiously (this was necessary),
and, in an hour, a dozen were bagged. There
was only this disadvantage. The wood was so
large, the smoots so far apart, that many
of the hares screamed for some seconds before
they could be dispatched. The continuance
of this screaming brought up the keepers, and
our game was up, and with it what we had
bagged. The watchers numbered four or five,
and, leaving everything, we ran. In our line
of retreat was an abandoned hut built by the
charcoal burners, consisting of poles, with
heather and fern for roof and sides. We made
for this, hoping, in the darkness, to elude
our pursuers, then double in our tracks
as soon as they had passed. But they were
not so easily deceived. As soon as the
crackling of the dead sticks caused by our
tread had ceased, they evidently suspected
some trick, and knew that we were still in the
wood. And the hut was the first object of

search. As they were quite unaware of our number they declined to enter, but invited us into the open. We replied by barricading the narrow doorway with poles and planks which we found within. Of course this was only completing our imprisonment, but we felt that one or more of their number would be sent for fnrther help, and that then we would make a dash to escape. We agreed to take off in different directions, to divide the attacking force, and then lead them across the roughest country we could find. A deep stream was not far off, and here we would probably escape. But our scheme went wrong—or, rather, we had no opportunity to put it into practice. After waiting and listening awhile we saw lights glisten in the chinks of the heather walls, and then fumes of smoke began to creep up them. They were burning us out. Quietly as we could we undid the barricading, and, as the air rushed in, tiny tongues of flame shot up the heather. Now we lay low with our faces on the damp floor. Then a pole was thrust through. Another current of air and the flames shot everywhere. The thick smoke nearly stifled us, and the heat became intense. The fire ran up the poles, and burning bits of the heather roof began to fall. Then came the crisis. A fir pole had been raised without, and then was to crash through the hut. This was the first outside proceeding we had seen—we saw it through the riddled walls. As soon as the men loosed their hold of the tree for its fall we sprang from the doorway ; and then for a few seconds the sight was magnificent. As the roof crashed in the whole hut was one bright mass of flame, and a sheet of fire shot upwards into the night. The burning brackens and ling sent out myriads of sparks, and these falling around gave us a few seconds' start. As agreed, we each hurled a burning brand among the keepers, then disappeared in the darkness. Certainly no one followed us out of the wood. We had simply scored by lying low with the fire about us, taking advantage of the confusion and dazzling light, and then knowing our way out of the difficulty. The squire's son, we saw, was one

of the attacking party. We were a bit burnt, we lost the game and nets, but were quite content to have escaped so easily.

There is another incident which I have good cause to remember all my life. It is of a somewhat different nature to the foregoing, and occurred on the estuary of the river which I used frequently to net with good results. Someone who was certainly not very friendly disposed had seen me and my companion start for our fishing ground, and had made the most of their knowledge. After getting to the near vicinity of our work, we lay down beneath a hay-rick to wait for a degree of darkness. Then we crawled on hands and knees by the side of a fence until it brought us to a familiar pool which we knew to be well stocked with salmon and trout. As we surveyed the water we heard voices, and knew that the pool was watched. These sounds seemed to come from the lower limbs of a big tree, and soon one of the watchers hidden in the branches stupidly struck a match to light his pipe. This not only frescoed two forms against the night, but

lit up their faces with a red glow. The dis-
covery was a stroke of luck. We knew where
we had the water bailiffs, and the rest was easy.
We got quietly away from the spot, and soon
were at work in a pool further up stream.
No one but a gaunt heron objected to our
fishing, and we made a splendid haul. The
salmon and sea-trout had begun to run,
and swarmed everywhere along the reaches.
We hid our net in the "otter" holes, and,
under heavy loads, made for home across the
meadows. We were well aware that the local
police changed duty at six in the morning, and
timed our entry into town precisely at that
hour. But our absence of the previous night
had gone further abroad, and the local Angling
Association, the Conservancy Board, and the
police had each interested themselves in our
doings. It was quite unsafe to hide the spoil,
as was usual, and home it must be carried. I
was now alone. In the open I felt com-
paratively safe, but as I neared my destination
I knew not whom I should meet round the
next turn. Presently, however, it seemed as

though I was in luck. Every wall, every hedgerow, every mound aided my going. Now a dash across an open field would land me almost at my own door. Then I should be safe. I had hardly had time to congratulate myself on my getting in unobserved when a constable, then a second, and a third were all tearing down upon me from watch points, where they had been in hiding. The odds were against me, but I grasped my load desperately, drew it tightly upon my shoulders, and ran. The police had thrown down their capes, and were rapidly gaining upon me. I got into a long slouching trot, however, determined to make a desperate effort to get in, where I should have been safe. This they knew. Strong and fleet as I was I was too heavily handicapped, but I felt that even though I fell exhausted on the other side of the door-way, I would gain it. My pursuers—all heavy men— were blown, and in trouble, and I knew there was now no obstacle before me. Now it was only a distance of twenty yards—now a dozen. The great thuds of the men's feet were close

M

upon me, and they breathed like beaten horses. My legs trembled beneath me, and I was blinded by perspiration. "Seize him," "seize him," gasped the sergeant—but I was only a yard from the door. With a desperate feeling that I had won, I grasped the handle and threw my whole weight and that of my load against the door, only to find it—locked. I fell back on to the stones, and the stern chase was ended.

For a minute nobody spoke—nobody was able to. I lay where I fell, and the men leaned against what was nearest them. Then the sergeant condescended to say " poor beggar"—and we all moved off. The fish were turned out on the grass in the police station yard, and were a sight to see. There were ninety trout, thirty-seven salmon-morts, and two salmon. I was not detained. One of the men handed me a mort, telling me I would be ready for a substantial breakfast. I knew what it all meant, and first thought of bolting, then settled that I would do as I had always done—face it out.

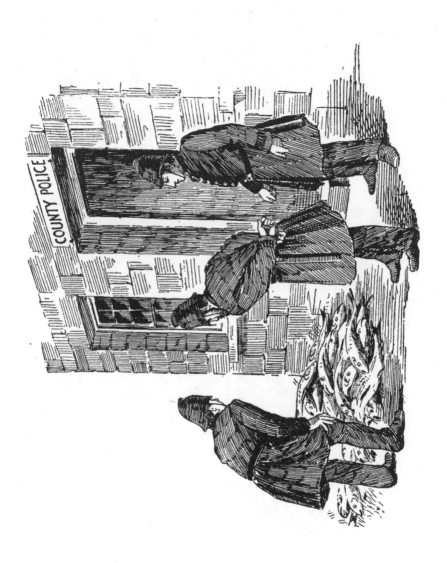

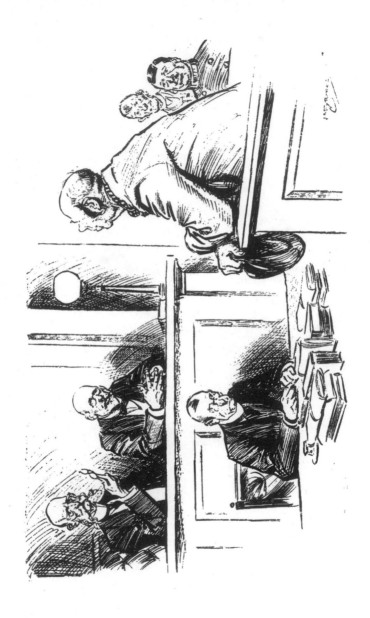

But I little knew what this meant, as will presently be seen. I knew sufficient of the law to forsee that I should be charged with trespassing ; with night poaching ; with being in illegal possession of fish ; with illegally kiiling and taking salmon ; perhaps other counts besides. But what I did *not* know was that I should be charged, in addition, with being in illegal possession of one hundred and twenty-nine salmon and trout *during the close season.*

And this is how it came about. There had been an agitation throughout the whole of the Conservancy district. It was contended that the fishing season extended too far into Autumn by a fortnight—that by that time the fish had begun to spawn. The old condition of things had held for years, and the new Conservancy bye-laws had only just come into operation. And so I was trapped. The case came on, and a great shoal of magistrates with it. Two of them were personally interested, and were charitable enough to retire from the Bench —they pushed their chairs back about an inch from the table. I pleaded guilty to all the charges except the last, and explained the case as clearly as I could. The Conservancy solicitor, who prosecuted, did then what he had never done before. It was a bad case he said, but added that I had never before been charged with netting during "close-time," and had never used lime or other wholesale methods of poisoning. He pointed out, too, to the presiding Justice that I always claimed to "poach square"—at which all the young ones laughed. He did not press for the heaviest penalty. But this was quite unnecessary, as I got it without. I never quite understood how they made it up, but I was fined ninety-seven pounds. I told the Chairman that I should pay it "in kind," and went to "hard" for nine months.

Other Victorian and Edwardian facsimile reprints from
Old House Books

Murray's Modern London 1860

Although essentially a guide for visitors this book is also an excellent read containing well written descriptions of pretty well everything a tourist might wish to know if he were visiting London a century and a half ago.

Packed with well researched facts and statistics we can wander around the streets, markets and fine buildings being told who lived where, what treasures may be found within, the volume of trade conducted in the markets, the number of patients in the hospitals and the courses available at universities and colleges. We also visit prisons, exhibitions, clubs and societies, residences of the famous, sites associated with remarkable events and witness the diverse commodities passing through the docks.

Much can also be learned about how daily life then differed from today. Some things were better such as the workings of the Post Office 'letters posted before 6 in the evening would be delivered the same evening within 3 miles'. But much was worse such as the appalling sewage arrangements. 'The daily discharge into the Thames would cover 36 acres to a depth of 6 feet' but already there was an understanding of pollution and sewage works were planned.

A jewel of a book for anyone wishing to explore London during the first half of Victoria's reign.

London Stories 1910

A cornucopia of anecdotal gems that allow us to wander through the past and meet some of the people who helped define the greatest city the world had ever seen. A collection of stories that originally appeared as magazine articles before the First World War which introduce us to a gathering of Londoners, both famous and forgotten, and tell of some of the extraordinary happenings and curiosities that coloured their lives.

We meet The Duke of Wellington's outspoken boot maker, the 'apple woman' who annexed Hyde Park and the recluse who weighed the world. We read of the curious wanderings of Cromwell's head, the semaphore system which sent signals from the Admiralty to Deal in less than a minute and a fatal duel fought in Kensington for the most absurd reason. We hear of a fire at Drury Lane Theatre, military executions in Hyde Park, visit Dr Johnson's favourite pub and read a letter to The Times that prompted the building of Nelson's column.

Old House Books, Moretonhampstead, Devon, TQ13 8PA. UK
www.OldHouseBooks.co.uk   info@OldHouseBooks.co.uk   01647 440707

Baedeker's London and its Environs 1900

This comprehensive guide takes us on a tour of the world's greatest city at the close of the Victorian era.

All major sites are described in detail. There are 33 walking tours including The City, St. Paul's, Regent's Park Zoo and London Docks and a dozen by river steamer and train including The Crystal Palace, Windsor Castle and as far afield as Rochester and St.Albans. Each is packed with directions, historical facts, travel arrangements and prices.

The advice on etiquette, security, accommodation, travel to and within Britain and recommended shops paint a fascinating picture of life a century ago. There is a history of London.

Over 500 pages, a fold out map, plans of notable buildings and 31 pages of coloured street plans, printed facsimile from the original edition. A source of fascination for anyone wishing to explore London a century ago.

The British Empire world map 1905

As the twentieth century dawned the British Empire enjoyed its heyday. This map shows British possessions coloured red at a time when it spanned eleven and a half million square miles with 400 million inhabitants.

This colour reproduction of a contemporary world map shows details of global trade, including: the furs of fox, bear, seal and otter brought from the shores of Canada's Lake Athabasca by canoes in summer and dog sleds in winter; cochineal, indigo and vanilla from central America; teak and bamboo from Siam; cinnamon and pearls from Ceylon; tortoise shells and birds of paradise from New Guinea as well as minerals and foodstuffs from all over the world. In the Sahara we note that slaves were still being traded. Four other maps show the development of the empire in the previous four hundred years.

Coaling stations, telegraph cables, railways and caravan routes are all marked. A ten-page gazetteer describes over 200 British countries and possessions as well as 33 (including Normandy and the USA) which had been lost to the crown.

Old House Books, Moretonhampstead, Devon, TQ13 8PA. UK
www.OldHouseBooks.co.uk   info@OldHouseBooks.co.uk   01647 440707

A Street Map of London, 1843

One of the earliest detailed street maps of London published over a century and a half ago so that passengers in Hansom cabs could check that they were being taken by the shortest route.

Faithfully reproducing the original hand colouring, it shows street names, prominent buildings, docks, factories, canals and the earliest railways in minute detail.

Beyond the limits of the developed area, which in 1843 extended no further than Hyde Park in the west and Stepney in the east, can be seen the orchards and market gardens of Chelsea and Southwark, the marshes of the Isle of Dogs and the outlying villages of Earls Court, Kentish Town and Bow.

Each map is accompanied by a history of London in 1843 which helps to set the scene as you embark on your journey through the greatest city in the world early in the reign of Queen Victoria.

Compare this map to Bacon's Map of London 1902 to see the massive development that took place during the Victorian era.

Bacon's Up to date map of London, 1902

The reign of no other monarch saw such extensive change as that which took place when Queen Victoria was on the throne. This street map of London originally published at the end of her long life provides a perfect contrast with the map of London 1843. Gone are the orchards of Chelsea and the marshes of The Isle of Dogs. Earl's Court and other villages lying beyond the built up area at the beginning of her reign have now been swallowed by the expanding conurbation.

There is extensive development and activity on the lower reaches of the Thames where there is much evidence of the new docks servicing the needs of both the Empire and the mother country.

Many of the underground railway lines we know today have already been built. But there was much more to be completed during the coming century and places such as Willesden and Herne Hill were still surrounded by countryside in 1902.

Old House Books, Moretonhampstead, Devon, TQ13 8PA. UK
www.OldHouseBooks.co.uk   info@OldHouseBooks.co.uk   01647 440707

Dickens's Dictionary of London, 1888

An unconventional Victorian guidebook which vividly captures the atmosphere and vitality of what was then the largest city in the world, the heart, not just of the nation, but also of a great empire. Through a series of over 700 detailed entries contained in 272 pages printed facsimile from the original 1888 edition, we build up a living portrait of Victorian London, from the fashionable gentlemen's clubs of St James's to the markets and slums of the East End. 1888 was the year of the Jack the Ripper murders. The remarks on the principal buildings, the churches and the great railway stations, the banks, theatres and sporting facilities are informative and well observed, the comments of someone who obviously knew London like the back of his hand.

Equally revealing and very entertaining are the wealth of tips on social behaviour. There is essential advice on everything from the hiring of servants (a parlour maid's recommended salary was £12 per annum), the benefits of cycling (most welcome in view of the saving of cruelty to horseflesh), how to cope with milk contaminated with diphtheria and typhoid, fogs (much appreciated by the predatory classes) through to avoiding the attention of carriage thieves.

Dickens's Dictionary of The Thames, 1887

A fascinating portrait of the river at the height of its Victorian prosperity. On the upper Thames it was the carefree era of regattas and riverside picnics, while London's tideway and great docks were busy with the comings and goings of barges, steamers and sailing ships servicing the world's largest port and the Empire on which the sun never set.

This treasure trove of a book has descriptions of the villages and towns along the river from its source near Cricklade to the Nore Lightship. It is packed with practical advice, maps of popular destinations, locations of angling and bathing spots. Riverside inns to accommodate oarsmen are listed with details of how to return boats by train at a time when an annual season ticket between Windsor and Paddington cost as little as £18.

Old House Books, Moretonhampstead, Devon, TQ13 8PA. UK
www.OldHouseBooks.co.uk   info@OldHouseBooks.co.uk   01647 440707

*Other Victorian and Edwardian facsimile reprints from
Old House Books*

Oarsman's & Angler's Thames map, 1893

Explore Britain's best loved waterway with the map that must surely have been used by the *Three Men in a Boat*. Very detailed, one inch to the mile and over 8 feet in length, it shows all 164 miles from the source to London Bridge. Riverside towns and villages are marked with historical information and details of the locks and how to operate them.

For fishermen, the best pools where trout, pike, perch and others were to be found. There are also details of toll charges and angling laws and a description of life on the river over a century ago when the Thames was the nation's favourite place for recreation and sport with as many as 30,000 anglers and 12,000 small boats regularly using the river. The Great Western and Southern Railways delivered hordes of Londoners to the area for steamer trips, regattas and riverside picnics.

The English Companion

In this witty and stylish companion to Englishness Sunday Times columnist Godfrey Smith takes us on a leisurely but perceptive tour of all that he holds dear in England and the English. It is very much an informal ramble, as if in the company of an old friend. He treats us to a display of sparkling and knowledgeable comments on our national life from Churchill to Pubs, Elgar to Rugby, Bertie Wooster to George Orwell, British Beef to the National Lottery and from Fish and Chips to Evelyn Waugh.

'A most entertaining book' Kingsley Amis

'A mixture of eccentricity & scholarship, highly entertaining' A.J.P.Taylor

*Old House Books, Moretonhampstead, Devon, TQ13 8PA. UK
www.OldHouseBooks.co.uk info@OldHouseBooks.co.uk 01647 440707*

Other Victorian and Edwardian facsimile reprints from
Old House Books

Enquire Within upon everything 1890

In the wake of the Industrial Revolution the population swiftly developed a thirst for knowledge about the myriad of new goods and ideas that were becoming available. But before the days of television, newspaper advertising and junk mail how did people get to know about everything? Over a million people solved the problem by buying a copy of this book which caused a publishing sensation in Victorian Britain. Because it explained so much about so many different aspects of life it continues to provide a very enjoyable peep into the lifestyle of our forebears.

In 2775 entries the enquiring Victorian learns to tell if food is fresh and when it is in season; the rules of games and puzzles; how to dance; the difference between dialects; correcting grammar and spelling; hints on etiquette; kitchen and household hints and recipes; cures for scores of ailments including rheumatism and baldness; the origins of Christian names; first aid; employment and rental regulations; keeping fit; dressmaking and embroidery; births, marriages and deaths; personal conduct as well as scores of others.

Many of the gems in this book are now so well known that it seems incredible that they ever required explanation but there was still much more to be done and we find that all sorts of potions, cures and tinctures still had to be prepared at home. The days of 'off the shelf' and 'ready to use' had not yet arrived.

This book was originally published to tell people about the rapidly changing present. Now it serves to tell us about the rapidly receding past.

Old House Books, Moretonhampstead, Devon, TQ13 8PA. UK
www.OldHouseBooks.co.uk   info@OldHouseBooks.co.uk   01647 440707